# Do-It-Yourself Vacation Rental Branding

By Dana Susan Beasley;
with Deborah S. Nelson

Volume 2: Vacation Rental Owner's Manual

Published by DS Publishing, 3107 West Colorado Avenue #303,
Colorado Springs, CO 80904-2040, support@DSPublishing.biz www.DSPublishing.info

# Table of Contents

## Disclaimer

Please note much of this publication is based on personal business experience and anecdotal evidence and the author assumes no responsibility for errors or omissions. Also, you may use this information as you see fit, and at your own risk. There are no guarantees as to the success of any of the information contained herein either in part or as a whole. Your particular situation may not be exactly suited to the examples illustrated here; in fact, it's likely that they won't be the same, and you may adjust your use of the information and recommendations accordingly. Any trademarks, service marks, product names, or named features are assumed to be the property of their respective owners, and are used only for reference. There is no implied endorsement if we use one of these terms.

# Introduction
## Do-It-Yourself Vacation Rental Branding

So you've decided to turn your home into a vacation rental. You've bought the linens, hired the cleaning crew, listed your place with a listing on Vacation Rental by Owner—VRBO.com—and you're ready to go.

Think again. Your vacation rental is a business, and in order to treat it as a business, you need to treat it seriously. Face it. On the Internet, image is everything. Your prospects will only look at your site for a few seconds before they make a decision to stay or to go. Their decision is based on first impressions. And if you don't have a brand that distinguishes you from other vacation rentals, you will receive only a limited amount of bookings.

On sites like VRBO.com your property is competing against thousands upon thousands of other vacation rentals. There's also indirect competition like B&Bs and hotels. Think about it. Your prospects are going to be skeptical. Most likely they have heard of vacation rental scams. Some of your prospects are going to be downright scared. Unlike the reliability of a national brand like Holiday Inn, your vacation rental business is an unknown entity. And an unknown entity is full of danger. Buyer beware, indeed.

You entered into the vacation rental business to be outrageously busy. You want your home to have little or no vacancies. You want to make a profit! But are your bookings falling flat of expectations? How do you soar above the competition and get noticed? You do it by building a brand for your vacation rental! But what is a brand? A brand is an image or identity that captures the essence of your identity—who you are as a vacation rental business. It includes a logo mark and your vacation rental home name. Be prepared to build a brand that gets noticed and to unmask once and for all your authentic brand identity! Then your vacation rental bookings will soar!

By reading this book, you are beginning an exciting quest! As you follow my carefully laid out action steps included at the end of each chapter, you will watch your vacation rental brand develop before your eyes! And you will have avoided the expensive task of hiring it out! This is truly do-it-yourself!

Through this book, you will discover an image unique to you and your vacation rental business because it will be authentically you, not just smoke and mirrors or gimmicks, but a brand that will capture what your vacation home is truly about and what you are truly about.

I will be guiding you through a step-by-step process of building your brand and then I will show you how to strategically market that brand. You will discover your unique vacation rental identity. This includes a logo, slogan, and much, much more, all guided from my perspective and experience as a graphic artist, Internet publisher, and vacation rental owner.

### Why Create a Unique Logo/Brand?

Why create a unique brand/logo design? The reason is that in order to communicate trustworthiness, you need a brand strategy that is consistent across all mediums, both online and offline. You need to build brand visibility for your home, whether that's on a listing, a blog, your Website, or signage on your door!

Freebies and low-cost printing solutions like Vistaprint may be an easy solution to getting started, but if you're serious about building a successful vacation rental, you need more than a unique logo. You will need a compelling brand.

Brands get noticed. Think about McDonald's. What child doesn't recognize the symbol of the golden arches? What serious coffee drinker can't recognize the Starbuck's logo? Or how about Kleenex? It is a household word now, so much so that all tissues are generally called Kleenex. If your vacation rental business is not important to you, it will be reflected in your image. You actually hurt your business in the long run with no branding strategy.  As a matter of fact, a brand is a company's most valuable asset.

Free logos and logos designed by non-professionals may not be tailored to your vacation rental and target market. You will not get the results you want! But as a professional graphic artist, Internet marketer, and vacation rental owner, I am going to share with you the secrets of building not only a logo and a brand, but a brand strategy that will get you noticed! You will soar above the competition and increase your bookings!

## Who Am I Anyway?

Now you may be asking; who am I anyway? As a professional graphic artist, I have been designing logos and brands that get noticed for over 17 years, first as part of a communications agency for a non-profit, then as a freelance designer, and most recently as the publisher of Internet marketing materials, including Volume 1 of Vacation Rental Owner's Manual. My logo designs have received so much notice that I won a contest for a balloon festival in Colorado, and as part of my prize, I got to ride in a hot air balloon! I definitely took my company, AngelArts, to new heights that day!

Now I am excited to help you build an effective brand for your vacation rental. With my help, you will create a do-it yourself brand that will get noticed and result in increased bookings!

## Expectations

In this book, you will receive:

- A step-by-step guide to developing your vacation rental brand
- Easy—to- understand instructions
- Action-oriented assignments
- Examples and stories of effective brands

What makes an effective brand strategy? Building your brand across online and offline mediums. Online branding encompasses the Internet (including listing sites like VRBO.com). Offline brand-building includes postcards, brochures, business cards, signage, and promotional products. (You will learn more about developing effective promotional products in Chapter Six).These avenues give your target market a sense of trust. They build an affinity with your potential guests which will result in more bookings!

When you build a brand, you can turn that brand into a product. Then you can sell your branded products in your own vacation rental home, make money, and advertise your business at the same time! When you learn to create a unique design that stands out and screams professionalism, you become more successful at reaching your goals for your business. In other words, your bottom line improves!

Building a brand that gets noticed—building it from your specific passions, mission, and vision—is more effective than putting up a "pretty logo." The logo is only part of your brand. Because your brand is you, you will want to make it as authentic to your mission and passion as possible.

*A caveat about the step-by-step creative process is that it is hard to break down into chronological order. Often when an idea sparks, it also sparks many other ideas all at once. If that happens to you and you want to start by making sketches or playing on your software, great! It's kind of like dancing. You have to learn all the steps in order, but once you learn, the actual move is as smooth as silk! That's why a pro makes it look so easy!*

Actually, your brand will be most effective when perception meets reality. Think of all those marketing consultants out there who try to manipulate prospects into buying a product based on image. But when the product doesn't measure up to the image, the brand fails, and the company becomes "branded" in a negative way!

So are you ready to go on this quest to unmask your authentic vacation rental business identity? Keep reading and applying yourself diligently to the assignments and in no time at all you will be building a brand that gets noticed and which will result in increased bookings!

# Chapter One

## Create a Vision of Your Brand in Less Than 24 Hours!

**More Advantages**

I know you can't wait to get started, so I'm going to show you how you can craft a vision of your vacation rental brand in less than 24 hours! You are not only going to craft a vision of your brand, you are going to craft a vision of your life and business.

Why a vision of your life, not just a brand? Because the more clarity you have for your life and business, the more clarity you have about what you are called to be and do. The vision you craft will make a real difference to your guests. Isn't that why you became a vacation rental owner?

For us, creating a business was so much more than making money. Yes we needed to make money, but we also wanted to provide a valuable service to others by offering our home to strangers. As vacation rental business owners, it was gratifying to provide a cozy place for military families to stay.

When you know about your unique strengths and callings, you will have confidence and focus. Focus like a laser on what makes you unique. When you know this information, you can put it into your brand. And then your brand will get noticed!

Go to a quiet place where you can think and write and dream. Eliminate all distractions. This will probably take you less than hour; maybe more, depending on how detailed you are. Remember that you are brainstorming. There are no right or wrong answers. This is a time to really dig deep. To help you I will be asking some questions that you may think, "What does that have to do with a brand or my vacation rental business?" They may seem general, but they are very important.

Because you are the brand, the most important question you can ask is, "What is my why?" And to do that, you need to thoroughly examine everything about your goals and passions. You are a unique person and you bring uniqueness to your vacation rental business! When you let your uniqueness shine through to your brand, it will get noticed!

You want to have a clear vision of who you are and where you are going. When your image is based on reality, not just perceptions, then your brand will soar above the competition! This is a process and a journey, so I've come up with 20 questions I've asked myself and answered over the period of many years. I keep refining my vision, and the more clarity I gain through this process, the better able I am to focus on what's really important. In some cases I've asked several questions on one topic to get your mind active and engaged.

You may want to get a special three-ring binder for journaling to keep you organized as you go through this book.

# Identity Questions

1 What are your life experiences? Write a story about an accomplishment that had a profound impact on your life. You can write more than one if you like. After you write the story or stories, ask yourself how these accomplishments translate to skills and talents that you uniquely possess? Also, write a story of an accomplishment in your vacation rental business. How did your home help your guest? How did you feel about that?

2 What do you value? What are your guiding principles in life and n your vacation rental business? What is important to you? Not important to you?

3 What skills have you acquired? Be sure to use action verbs.

4 What are your gifts? What are your talents?

5 What are your character qualities?

6 What is your personality like? (This will help you make key decisions such as the kind of work environment that helps you to be the most productive—structured or flexible? You can take a Myers-Briggs test to find out what your personality is generally like.)

7 Do you have any special needs or challenges you need to be aware of? For instance, are you dyslexic, ADHD, etc.? What are the obstacles and how can you overcome them?

8 What are your goals for your life? What are your goals for your vacation rental business? What is your desired result of your life and business?

9 What are your goals for the next 20 years? What is your desired result?

10 What are your goals for the next 10 years? Five years? What is your desired result?

11 What are your goals for the next year? What is your desired result?

12 What do you hope to get out of this book?

13 What is the purpose of your life? Of your vacation rental business? What is the reason for your existence? For the existence of your business?

14 What is the mission of your life? Of your business? What is the aim of your life?

15 What are you passionate about? What gets your blood going? What motivates you to get out of bed in the morning? What thoughts keep you up at night? What makes your eyes light up when you talk about it?

16 What is the vision of your life? A morbid way to ask this question is to think ahead to your funeral. What do you want people to say about you? That you spent all your time working? What kind of impact do you want to have on people, especially through your vacation rental business?

17 What is your vacation rental business vision? What do you want it to look like?

18 When you think about it in the future, how do you imagine it?

19 What are your strengths? What are you good at? What are your weaknesses? What are you not so good at?

Now that you've gone through these 19 questions, here's the most relevant question of all (and I will be asking it again):

20 What is the number one point you want to make with a new vacation rental brand identity?

# Assignment

- [ ] 1 Get a three-ring binder to hold all your assignments. Put in some extra paper—both blank, lined, and perhaps graph paper—for note taking, sketching, and journaling.

- [ ] 2 Answer the 20 questions on the previous pages, by copying the pages and writing them out by hand or writing them directly in this book.

# Chapter Two

## Definitions You Must Know to Get Started

To click or not to click, that is the question—on the Internet, that is. Your ultimate goal is to either make a sale or to capture an interested person's email when they click on your Website. After all, you are facing extreme competition from a site like VRBO.com and other listing sites.

What causes a prospect to click on your image and not another? The answer is "strategic branding." You have maybe 10 to 30 seconds to make that all-important first impression that leads to a desired action such as having the client click on the link to your Website or call you to make a booking. That's why a compelling brand specifically tailored to your target market is so important.

But what exactly is a brand? What's the difference between a brand and a logo? What's a slogan? And what in the world is a business identity? These terms need to be defined so you can create a strategic brand that will get noticed immediately and that will lead to the clicks or phone calls you desire from your prospect!

### What is a Logo?

A logo is an identifying mark: a way of distinguishing your vacation rental business from your competition, whether direct or indirect. A logo captures a person's eye, draws them into what you are as an entity, and what you are promoting—specifically, your home. A logo shows and demonstrates what you are about and what your target market can expect.

Logos are applied to what you're selling or promoting to give that person a picture instead of just a name full of letters. A logo is a simple mark or symbol, usually with type, illustrations, and/or photographs that identify your business. A logo sometimes refers to just the symbol or to both the symbol and business name. Not all logos use a symbol or mark. Some consist of just the words of the entity name. That is, in itself, the symbol or mark. It is called a "logotype."

Logos are used on identity collateral, such as business cards, stationery, brochures, return envelopes, and labels. They are also used on mediums such as Websites, blogs, print design, social marketing, and video marketing. Just think about the world's most recognizable logos. Here are some that come to the top of my mind:

- Holiday Inn—What traveler doesn't know about them?
- McDonald's—What child doesn't recognize the golden arches?
- Apple computers—The Apple Macintosh is ubiquitous these days with iPods, iPhones, and now iPads.
- Starbucks—Just picturing the logo makes me want to get a coffee!

Logos are all around us, all the time. Here are 10 logos I saw just today:

- Kroger Brand—now this is interesting, I search out this brand at my grocery store because I know it is not a major store brand. I feel when I buy Kroger products, that I am getting affordable value.
- St. Ives
- Apple Computer
- Tide
- Quaker Oats
- UPS Store
- Canon
- Brother
- Dodge
- YMCA

And last week as of this writing we stayed at a Best Western hotel! Talk about branding!

The above is by no means an exhaustive list of all the logos I encounter on a daily basis. Logos are all around us in their various shapes, sizes, and colors. Logos are an important part of our lives and extremely important for a business, including vacation rentals.

Logo marks, according to Rose DeNeve in her book, *The Designer's Guide to Creating Corporate ID Systems:*

> *... identify products and services, differentiating the company and its businesses from others in the field. They succinctly communicate the company's personality and culture. By serving as an endorsement, they add value to products and services. And they are legal properties that can be controlled and developed over time.*[1]

With today's Internet usage, social networking, and online vacation rental listing sites, logos are even more vital to a healthy business. Getting instant recognition is the job of a logo, which is a key to any branding program.

Like a cliché heard over and over again, logo symbols can be overused. After a while, they lose meaning because of heavy imitation by competitors and then you're right where you started—indistinguishable from any other company out there!

How do you avoid these pitfalls? We'll cover that in later chapters, so keep reading!

### My Logo

Let me tell you a little bit about how I designed the graphic part of my logos. First, I will tell you about my vacation rental logo. My husband and I owned and restored a historic Victorian home and we turned it into a vacation rental. Victorian decorating is my passion, so I incorporated it into our logo. The whole house was decorated with this theme.

I used a painting of Victorian roses as the graphic and put our rental home's name, Victorian Rose, in romantic lettering. This captured the essence of what our house was about.

The story about my publishing business logo is a little different. Over 10 years ago, I decided to teach music lessons. I had a picture of myself as a little baby reaching up to a piano keyboard. I was dressed in a white gown and my mother put a halo on me because it was Christmas time. So, I called my business "AngelMusic." A year or so later I decided to publish greeting cards with original art and text. I expanded my business into "AngelArts."

I scanned my picture, a simple black and white photograph, and surrounded it with a cloud frame to signify reaching to heaven. I made the frame pink because I am feminine and like frills. That's what makes me unique as a person and as a business. I love designs that are complicated, beautiful, and soft. Since my target market is mostly women, I know that being feminine is a good thing. I wanted to attract a like-minded audience.

### What is Identity?

Identity is what makes your vacation rental business unique. It captures the essence of your service and communicates the relevance of your brand's need, want, or desire to a target audience. Often in business terms this concept is referred to as a "corporate" or "business" identity. It is who you are represented in a graphic expression. It is your very essence—your unique selling proposition communicated in an image.

Identity consists of both logo mark and company (or in your case, rental property) name. It is how a company graphically distinguishes itself from the competition in the marketplace.

The company name is the single most important factor when creating an identity. A business identity encompasses not only the essence of the business it represents, but the emotions and associations the image brings up to a target audience.

What are examples of identity we see every day? Well, think of the emotions behind a logo:

- The cutting-edge, user-friendly products of Apple.
- The amazing social connections Facebook brings.
- The fun time McDonald's provides for children, no matter what adults think of their food!
- To some, the reliability and standard service of a Holiday Inn.

When I created my identity, AngelArts, I wanted an image that connoted inspiration, an image that captured the very essence of who I am. I am an artist who wants to reach new heights in her life. And I want my products and services to help others do the same. I wanted my identity to capture my mission which is that my art be a vehicle for God's glory. That is why I chose the photo in combination with company name, font choices, colors, and my slogan. (I will talk about slogans in a bit.) All of these choices combined graphically represent my identity as a business.

As far as my vacation rental business, I developed a simple logo to reflect what made our house unique—a beautiful Victorian home full of original art! This theme was echoed in everything we did, from a welcome letter to our Website to our guest book to the whole house.

### What's a Brand?

- A brand is a logo mark that is consistently and strategically applied across all mediums (print, Websites, social marketing, etc.) to assist target audiences in instantly identifying a business, organization, or artist.
- A brand stands for the development of a trusted relationship between the brand holder and the customer.
- A brand builds name recognition. It grows in value over time as that brand gains target market awareness, visibility, and reputation.
- A brand is a source of pride for a business. It is who you are and what you stand for and how you relate to the world.
- A brand creates a choice for guests. A recognized brand is familiar, safe. It says to a prospective customer, "I know you," and it promises satisfaction to him. When a customer

buys into a brand, it is because that brand stands on a foundation of trust rooted in the past, sustained in the present, and promised for the future. It is a promise of satisfaction made and kept.

- A brand is a lifelong companion, a living psychological entity in a customer's mind and heart.

Think about the brand of LaQuinta or The Marriott or even Motel 6. Each of these brands has a target market and a theme. The brands communicate the essence of what the company is and whom they serve. A successful brand has a higher price premium because of the customer's view that the brand brings satisfaction and familiarity.

Why, after all, do people stay in the same hotel trip after trip? Because the hotel is a known entity and a known entity is more comfortable emotionally!

A good brand identifies with the service offered to a prospect and conveys a consistent message across all mediums. A good brand tells a story. A brand can become a cultural icon. It actually bonds a target market to its image, almost creating a kinship between them.

## The Differences Between Identity, Brand, and Logo

What is the difference between identity, brand, and a logo? Unlike a business or corporate identity, which is the essence of who and what that company is, a brand is inherently tied to its product or service. A logo is the graphical representation of this identity and brand. And a brand is a type of product or service manufactured or offered by a business. It is also an identifying mark.

Think about the branding of cattle (after all this is the origin of the concept of branding). When ranchers brand cattle, they do it to protect their property. They are proclaiming to the other ranchers that they retain ownership of that particular steer or heifer. And what do they use to brand their cattle? An identifying mark—a symbol that represents the name of their ranch. It is a logo that communicates the name of the owner. They burn the symbol into their cattle's hide to identity the cattle as theirs.

These brands build awareness in the communities where the ranchers live. The rancher's cattle were distinct from those of other ranchers. In the same way, a brand of a vacation rental business builds awareness of that service. It creates familiarity with the distinctive qualities or the image of a vacation rental home.

When brands build customer recognition and awareness, they bring brand loyalty. Brand loyalty is the tendency of consumers to buy the same product repeatedly over that of a competing brand. Brands that are widely known have achieved brand leader status or brand name status. This is the enviable goal of any business, especially vacation rentals. Look how VRBO and Home Away have built their brands!

In recognition of this brand leader status, grocery stores like Kroger created their own generic brand! It communicates affordability, which creates a new kind of loyalty!

In contrast to a brand, an identity serves to establish who the owner of that brand is, by bearing that entity's name and other details such as a logo mark.

Think of a painter. A professional artist will sign her work with a distinguishing signature. This raises the value of the painting immediately. The identity of the painter is her name, represented by the mark. Building this professional emotion over time through providing a superb product (the painting), distinguished with the artist's mark, creates a bond with clientele—a brand.

Think of some more brands:

- Nike
- Vera Wang
- Canon
- Coca-Cola
- Pepsi

To whom are you loyal, Coca-Cola or Pepsi? Apple or Windows? Puffs or Kleenex?

Personally, I'm a Coca-Cola, Apple, Kleenex kind of gal! Why? Because these brands have proved their quality and reliability to me over and over again. Now, as far as hotels, I'm not too fond of them. They're all too beige for my taste. That's why I put so much thought into our vacation rental. It was based on years of staying in Bed & Breakfasts. Given the choice, I would much rather stay in a quaint B&B than a plain hotel.

Brands bring out strong emotions. I have a nephew by marriage who wouldn't even step into my office because it contained Macs. Obviously, he was completely loyal to the computers that run Windows operating software and shunned anything to do with Apple computers. Really, I feel the same way about Pepsi. I will choose Coke every time, and if I don't have a choice, most times I choose to drink nothing at all.

My identity, who I am, is AngelArts, a company that reaches new heights in life and beyond through the combining of excellent art and literature into products and services which homeschooling and work-at-home moms need, want, and desire. I captured this identity through my logo mark, the combination of my image (the photo of a little girl reaching up toward the piano) and typography (the fonts and color choices of my company name).

Over time, as I get my name and image out there, applying it consistently to different mediums, I will build brand awareness and recognition. When a prospect or customer sees my image repeatedly, she will say, "Oh, that's AngelArts. I can trust her products and services." In fact, I've had prospects tell me, "Oh, I know who you are! I saw you at such and such." Of course, a customer will only say that if I'm true to my identity, which includes quality and excellence; and if I make that brand visible through marketing—which I have. This is also what we did with our Victorian Rose brand. Both the online and offline marketing worked in synergy to build awareness about our vacation rental home.

A brand can also create customer dissatisfaction. Who can forget Coca-Cola's campaign of New Coke? They trotted this brand out in the 1980s and it tasted nowhere like the original! It was a complete botch! That's when they re-created the brand of original Coke. Their marketing did not match the quality of the new product. Think about this. If you open a vacation rental home and advertise your place as clean, and then it is not clean at all, your service will forever be negatively burned into the mind of your customer. This actually happened to us as guests in a vacation rental. It was dingy, dirty, and unpleasant. We left ahead of schedule. It did not meet our expectations and created dissatisfaction.

## What is a Slogan?

Many brands contain slogans or tag lines—a pithy saying that epitomizes what their brand offers. Who can forget, *"Just Do It?"* That slogan will be forever entwined with the Nike brand.

Of course, Home Away has their own slogan: *"Home Away from Home®."* We found out just how protective they are of that slogan! Take it from me, don't use it!

These days, a slogan or tag line could contain essential keywords for Site Engine Optimization (SEO) for a blog or Website or vacation rental listing site.

A slogan is like an elevator pitch. It is concise, to the point, and gets a message across in a few seconds. It creates end-user appeal to buy that brand.

I chose my slogan, *"Helping You Reach New Heights in Your Life and Beyond,"* because this captures the essence of how I can solve the problems of my customer. This slogan reflects back to the image of the little girl in the picture. It reflects the essence of who I am and my company mission. I see the whole needs of my customer, so that's why on my AngelArts website I have expanded the slogan to a benefit statement: *"Reach New Heights in Your Life, Relationships, Home, Business, Ministry, Homeschooling, and Artistry."*

## What Is a Trademark?

A trademark is like a stamp. It is a graphic identity registered with a governmental agency. A trademark legally protects your brand, much as a copyright protects art. A business name can be protected, as well as a slogan. You can apply for a trademark yourself or hire a lawyer to apply for you. We will cover this topic later on in the book.

I'm sure you've seen the trademark symbol, ®. If I were to use the logos of the companies I mentioned above, I would have to use the symbol.

## What is a Target Market?

A target market is a group of prospects that a business identifies as their specific potential customers or clients. This is also called an "audience." This is who you are in business—your reason for existing. You exist to turn prospects into guests. And to turn guests into repeat guests who spread the word about your vacation rental.

A target market needs to be as specific as possible. If you aim at nothing, you will hit at nothing! Considerations like income level, age, education level, location, interests, gender, and role in life all come into play when identifying a target market. Another term for this is niche marketing, or affinity marketing.

Think about it. Who does Guess market to? Who is a big market in the clothing industry? Teenagers! When I have gone into a Guess store (only because a teenage girl dragged me in kicking and screaming), I can easily tell that their target market is teenagers! Certainly they do not market to an educated homeschooling mother like me!

When I first started to homeschool our son over three years ago, I saw the potential of target marketing. I realized that I could use my publishing knowledge to create products that home-school moms need, want, and desire. I then began to identify my market, based on affinity. I am a homeschooling mother who is passionate about entrepreneurship and inspirational art. And I want to reach other mothers who have a similar need and interest! These mothers and their families are who we eventually decided to target with our vacation rental. We also targeted military couples, and they became our single best source for longer term stays.

## What is a Branding Strategy?

A branding strategy is a plan for applying a brand across different mediums in order to gain exposure and credibility for a business. A branding strategy includes guidelines for how your brand image will be applied, whether through print or Web mediums. It is a plan to build brand awareness and name recognition and it is intricately associated with a marketing strategy.

Marketing experts say it takes seven exposures to make a sale. A branding strategy ensures that a company image gains visibility repeatedly to a prospect so lead capture and sales can be made, thus improving the bottom line! Corporations formalize this process, but as a home business owner and graphic artist, this is more intuitive for me than anything. I make sure my images are the same across all platforms, from business cards to email marketing. My task is to get my brand in front of people. That is where a business plan and marketing plan are essential.

### What is Identity Collateral?

Identity collateral is the specific medium to which your graphic image is applied. This could be an online or offline means of marketing. Offline, these consist of marketing materials such as business cards, stationery, labels, envelopes, brochures, flyers, postcards, signage, etc.

Although identity collateral does not traditionally include new Internet mediums, it is still a huge factor in today's business climate. These mediums could include your Website, VRBO listing, blog, Facebook page, Twitter account, email marketing, article marketing, and video channel. If your brand is consistently applied to both offline and online collateral, you will build name recognition and visibility!

Developing my offline identity collateral was one of the first things I did in my AngelArts business. I had custom business cards professionally printed. That is the most important piece of my identity collateral puzzle.

Early on, I developed postcards with my vacation rental logo applied to them. This became a very effective form of marketing for us. I used to have a canned Website for AngelArts that did not work at all. I now recognize the value of custom-made mediums and I stay away from templates like the plague. Or, if I have to use a template, I modify it so it fits my brand.

I will be sharing with you later on in the book my number one source of printing offline collateral, including my postcards, so watch for that in an upcoming chapter.

# Assignment

- [ ] 1 Notice the brands you use on a daily basis. What drew you to that brand? What emotions does that brand bring across to you? Are you loyal to that brand? Also notice the brands of both direct and indirect competition. What do they have in common? What makes them stand out from one another?

- [ ] 2 Collect your favorite brands. Your snail mailbox is a great source for this! Direct mailers really know how to market! Start a file for your favorite images, including logos/brands you find online, in your home, and in your mailbox. What is it about the brand that appeals to you? What message does it get across? What colors does it use? What images or symbols? Observe closely! You can also collect brands you dislike. Why don't you like them? The color? The font? The pictures? For your convenience, you can collect these in a clear envelope for your notebook.

# Chapter Three
## Your Vacation Rental Persona

If you have not decided upon a vacation rental name, then one of the first things you need to do is to decide what you will name your business. Now, because your business, as a vacation rental homeowner is descriptive in nature, you will want to choose a name based on a persona (see below in this chapter). Your vacation rental business name is the single most important component in designing or re-designing your brand.

What if you want to change your name? Read on to find guidance on why you should or should not overhaul your name. There will be more on this in subsequent chapters.

So what is a persona? What are the advantages of using a persona?

### Persona

A persona is a descriptive name of a business which captures the essence of that business. It is a name that communicates succinctly the unique selling proposition (USP) of that business. The name needs to strike at the heart of the character of that business. A persona brings up emotions. It is based on associations and connotations.

If conceived properly, a persona:

- Describes the heart of your business.
- Communicates the message of your business.
- Is easy to encapsulate in an image or symbol.

- Acts as a directory of products or services.[1]
- Contains words easily made into a picture.
- Is memorable.
- Can use keywords.
- Is marketing that is not based on ego but what you have to offer.
- Will help you create better marketing copy for your listings.

What are the cons of using a persona?

A persona:

- Is easy to create a name that doesn't identify with an audience.
- Has to be a good name or it will fail.

If you change focus or name, you will have to rebuild your brand. Even though you as a vacation rental homeowner will use a persona for your business name, you should still use your personal name as part of your brand. With online marketing, especially, it is important to "come out from behind the curtain" and show your prospects who you are.

The anonymity of the Internet can scare off customers afraid of scams, especially vacation rentals. The advantage of being a vacation rental business over being a corporation is that you can distinguish yourself above the faceless nature of big travel business. Yes, you can level the playing field. That's the gift of the World Wide Web!

Examples of personas in the "real world" include:

- Freedom Financial Services
- Petsmart
- Pottery Barn
- Blue Bunny ice cream
- Dish Network

When it comes to Internet marketing, one of my favorite companies is the Barefoot Executive aka Carrie Wilkerson. I love what this name conjures up in the mind—it truly describes the life of working at home!

Carrie Wilkerson went from almost $100,000 in debt to paying off all her debts. She is now a successful Internet marketer. She adopts children, cares for their special needs, and donates significantly to orphanages. Obviously, leveraging a persona has worked for her!

I already mentioned why I named our home Victorian Rose. It truly captured the descriptive nature of our home! I also chose a persona for my business name, AngelArts. Why? Because I wanted something descriptive I could depict through an image. I wanted a word that encapsulated my passion for the inspirational arts. I wanted a name that brought associations of reaching up into the heavens to achieve a higher goal.

### What If You Want to Change Your Name?

Maybe you want to really overhaul your brand, including a name change! So, when is this a good idea and when is it not?

What you need to do is a thorough analysis of your business. Is your name really communicating the essence of your vacation rental business? You might even want to do some market research. Is your audience "getting you" from your name or are they confused? When they stay at your home, is there a disconnect between what you promised them online and what they experienced? I will talk about the process of changing your name later on in the book.

# *Assignment*

- [ ] 1 Notice persona brands. What appeals to you about them? Are they effective? What are the brands' drawbacks? What emotions/associations do the brands bring up? How effectively does the logo reflect the company's persona?

- [ ] 2 Notice brands of vacation rentals. Look through the VRBO.com site and other vacation rental sites. Notice how some use a name for their homes and some don't. Notice how some use a profile picture and some don't. How do you think the absence of a name and profile picture would effect a buyer's decision to book a home?

# Chapter Four
## Essential Elements of a Well-Designed Logo/Brand

Understanding the elements that go into designing a logo/brand is an extremely important first step in building a brand that gets noticed. Pay close attention to all the information I am about to share. A keen awareness of these elements will practically guarantee that you will have a brand that stands out in the crowd.

If you decide to hire a graphic designer to create your logo, knowing the elements we are going to discuss in this chapter will save you much time, frustration, and money. You will be able to communicate more effectively to your designer, and, therefore, your logo will more accurately reflect your vacation rental business, making it more successful.

Even if you hire someone from Guru.com or 99Designs, you will be able to intelligently communicate the brand you need. This will result in a successful logo that gets you results. You will have spent your money wisely! In effect, you will be the art director, armed with the knowledge you need to make a brand that gets noticed!

How I wish my clients in the non-profit I worked for had this course when I designed logos and other marketing materials for them! When I worked for a nonprofit organization as a graphic designer in their communications department, there was a lack of understanding about brand building. So, I came up with this idea of educating business owners about the design process. Keep reading and be prepared to learn so your brand will be noticed!

## A Primer

A logo consists of two basic components:

- A business name
- A symbol or mark

The name of the business is expressed through this very important design element:

## Typography

Typography is an art in itself. Typography is the art of arranging typefaces (or fonts).

There is a lot more to typography than choosing a font. Besides typefaces, typography consists of spacing in, around, and between lines of type. Type also includes illustrations and marks.

Some brands actually consist of the founder's signature. Kind of reminds me of what professional fine artists do when they sign their works of art! The signature is in itself is a logo/brand! I mean, think about how much value Rembrandt's signature adds to an original painting!

Some logos only consist of the brand name laid out in a typographical font. I'm sure that in today's computer age, you are very familiar with fonts.

But do you know the three basic kinds of fonts? Do you know what the rule is about using fonts in a design? Keep reading to find out more!

What's the most important factor when choosing a typeface? Readability!

## Logo Marks

The logo mark usually consists of some type of photograph, illustration, or art. Sometimes, as I said, the logo mark is simply the name of the brand in a specific font.

But what's the most important factor when choosing elements for these components?

In any element, including typography used for a logo, readability and simplicity are key. These are your two golden rules when designing a logo: Whatever elements you choose, your logo must be readable and it must be simple because the main message has to get across to the intended audience or the logo is worthless.

Because creativity is the most important element of all, there are many rules of design which can be broken by an advanced designer, as long as the above criteria are met.

## Basic Elements

Here are some basic elements to keep in mind when designing your logo:

Contrast—The difference between light and dark tones.
Balance—How the elements are arranged in the design.
Composition/Proportion—Appealing is best. Unequal (not symmetrical) are usually the most appealing.
Shape—A rectangular shape is generally more appealing than a square shape.
Aestheticism—The above elements should be chosen based on what is aesthetic and appealing to the eye.
Weight—The most important element of the logo has to be the biggest or have the most weight. Not necessarily the biggest, but the element with the most emphasis. The element the eye is drawn to first.
Tone—A balance of high, low, and mid-tones or shades of gray.
Spacing—Elements need to be lined up vertically and horizontally. In other words, they can't just "hang out in space," but be grounded, like an axis.
Fonts—Two at the most. One sans serif or decorative, one serif (more on this later).
Colors—The use of color in a logo. Color is a very important element. Color sells, especially in today's Internet age. Colors mean things. For instance:

Red = excitement
Orange = passion, urgency
Blue = calmness

Purple = royalty
Yellow = happiness

## Most Important Element

Typography is the single most important element of your logo. Typography will be used in your business name and your slogan, if you choose to have one. Your typography choices will also influence your later decisions in designing identity collateral, marketing materials, and promotional products. Words convey meanings. Designing with type is a very important element in logo design because you are communicating a message and, hopefully, a call to action—such as a call to you to make a booking!

There are three basic types of typography:

- *Decorative*
- **Sans serif**
- Serif

Fonts are licensed and cost money. You can buy a collection of fonts on CD or on the Web. You will also find fonts already loaded on your computer, but the amount of fonts available for free on your computer is limited and they are often overused and amateur looking. I will share more about typography in a later chapter.

## Illustrations

Illustrations are original line drawings or computer drawings. Simple illustrations are often used with typography to create an effective logo. These illustrations, if made by hand, can be drawn in several different mediums, including:

| | | |
|---|---|---|
| Pen & Ink | Colored Pencils | Woodblocks |
| Markers | Acrylic | Watercolor |
| Chalk | Oil | Pastels |

Charcoal Mixed Media

Some elements apply to illustrations—composition, shading, resolution, contrast, and most importantly, relevancy to the topic of the logo. In other words, does the illustration enhance the message?

An illustration is a good idea for a vacation rental business. We used this method in some of our promotional products, like postcards. My husband, an architect, drew an illustration of the house and I designed it into postcards. We had these available for our guests to use. When they sent the card, it created brand recognition!

## Computer Drawings

These days many illustrations can be found by utilizing computer graphics. You can buy a whole collection from a service like Dreamstime.com. (I will talk more later about this great resource!) Clip art abounds on the Internet, but beware of clip art looking too cheesy, and be sure to check license agreements. On Dreamstime.com most of the art comes with a license to use for logos, but always check the fine print.

You can also make your own computer graphics using computer illustration software. Professional illustration software is an important tool for transforming logos into promotional products, such as embroidered shirts. I will share more about software in a future chapter.

Other sources of computer graphics include catalogs, your local Office Depot store, or even your own computer. But once again, make sure you have the legal right to use the graphics before you base your logo on it! Perhaps your best option for a logo image might be a photograph of your home. After all, that is what you are promoting!

## Photography

Photography can be used as a logo, but again, simplicity is paramount. Good photographs of your home are essential to your marketing. You must have clutter-free, crystal clear images of the front of your house and rooms. A good photograph of your home can serve as a very attractive logo. It makes good sense since that is what you are promoting—your home!

Another use of photography is a good photograph of yourself! In these days of Internet marketing, putting a face to your business will help build your credibility. You want a photograph to use on your VRBO listing Website, your email campaigns, your Facebook page, your blog, and your YouTube channel, if you have one. People are tired of faceless corporations. And scam artists are a dime a dozen. A photograph says to your prospect, "Oh, he's a real person!"

I was amazed after searching recently on VRBO for a little while how many owners did not have their photographs and names prominently displayed. This is one area where you can easily distinguish yourself! You immediately put your prospect at ease by showing that you are a real person.

Build your photograph into your brand and you will be building trust as you build your brand visibility. Internet marketing is about relationships. You can't do that without a picture. Make your picture visible on every Webpage, blog, email marketing piece, and everything!

The important elements of photography are:

Composition—How you fill the page.
Background—Nothing distracting, no sticks coming out of your head or undue clutter sitting around.
Lighting—Balance of lights and shadows. Don't use flash for your personal picture. Use "catch light." I'll cover more about this in another lesson.
Contrast—Vivid, striking colors—both dark and light tones in the image.
Angle—Looking down is usually the most flattering, especially for room shots.
Resolution—High setting for printing.

### Technical Considerations

What are the technical considerations for designing a logo? In a way, technical considerations are an element. Here is just enough information to get you started:

- Resolution—300 dpi (dots per inch) for print
- 72 dpi for Web

Many variations in these requirements exist for different production processes, for example, silk screening or embroidery.

### Color

- Computer screens are RGB (Red, Green, Blue).
- There are Web-safe colors, using hexadecimal color codes.
- Print is done using CMYK ink (Cyan, Magenta, Yellow, and Black). It is also called 4-color process or offset printing. This includes most digital color processes, although plates are not used for separation of colors, cutting down on the expense for short-run printing jobs. You can even add more colors to a full color process, such as metallic inks like gold or silver. Don't worry if you don't understand all this. I will cover more about printing processes in a later chapter.
- Spot color—One or more colors used in print design, silk screen, or embroidery. Metallic inks can be used for spot color, although this is more expensive. Spot color is used less often these days because of the convenience and affordability of digital printing. But spot color is used in some promotional products processes.
- Black and white or grayscale—The cheapest printing option, but with digital printing color is more affordable than ever. If you want to get noticed, you may want to use color. Although, if you have a striking black and white image, this in itself could make your logo stand out above the crowd!

### An Important Question

Let me suggest that you ask the printer this question. Will the logo be printed on paper? What kind of paper? What color paper? Why do you need to know this, especially if you plan on marketing primarily on the Internet?

Offline marketing is still very important! At the very least, you will want to create a business card for networking. You never know who you will run into in your sphere of influence. Don't create a logo without at least having this goal in mind for later. You might, as we did, want to create your own postcards for your guests' use. You may want to send thank you cards to your prospects after they inquire about your vacation rental.

Paper color is important. Your logo's characteristics will change with the color, texture, weight, and coating of your paper. There are some wonderful paper selections out there. Just take a trip to a local paper store like XPEDX. But all the beautiful choices aside, the most economical choice is white, which makes full-color coverage of your marketing materials and business collateral very attractive indeed.

**For the Web**—will your brand stand out? You have 10 to 30 seconds for a prospect to make a decision to click on your link. Is your logo compelling? Does it stand out from the background? It goes back to: is it readable, is it simple, does it convey accurately the message you want to convey? When you use these elements effectively, your brand will definitely stand out!

# Your Vision

So now that I've given you a broad view of the elements of your brand, begin envisioning what that brand would look like. What kind of typography will you use for your brand name? What image will you use for your logo mark, if any? Will it be an illustration, a computer drawing, or a photograph?

Draw a preliminary sketch below. It doesn't have to be perfect. You are not stuck with it. You are just trying to get an initial creative concept to get the ideas flowing. You will have more opportunities in later lessons to refine your vision and make it into a strategy.

# Assignment

- ❑ 1 Keep collecting brands you like and don't like. What fonts are used? What images? Are they computer drawings? Illustrations? Photographs? How complicated are these brands?

- ❑ 2 Draw an initial sketch on page 39.

# Chapter Five
## What to Do *After* the Brand Is Designed

In the last chapter, we covered a lot of territory on the essential elements that go into building your brand. But now what? This chapter will give you ideas on what to do with your brand once it's completed. Keep reading and don't forget to do your assignments at the end of each chapter. They will help you understand these strategies now so you know where you're heading. You will learn the best practices for online and offline marketing. You will also learn about promotional branded products, as well as the best formats and resolutions for your documents. You will wrap up the chapter by developing your own brand strategy. Ready to dive in?

### Brand Strategy

What will you do with your brand once you're finished building it? Promote it! And how do you promote it? Well, one of the first steps you will need to take is to create a brand strategy, or strategic marketing plan. This brand strategy needs to encompass both online and offline marketing methods. The goal of this branding strategy is to get your name and brand to as many people as possible and as many times as possible.

I've often heard it said that it takes at least seven repeated messages for a prospect to click on your link, subscribe to your newsletter, or buy your product. These messages are called "exposures." What you want to create is a plan of action. After all, why would you go to all the trouble of building your brand and then doing nothing with it?

There are basically three different types of marketing that I will be sharing with you. At the end of this lesson, I have provided a space where you can do some strategic planning. Get a bird's eye view now of what needs to be done and you will be ready to promote your brand when it's finished. Then your brand can truly sizzle!

## Online Marketing

Online marketing is the most exciting venue for brand promotion. If you are not online, then you will be left behind. It is hard to believe that any vacation rental business owner would not be taking full advantage of the Internet!

I heard it said recently that Google outsells the Yellow Pages! Many people, including myself, will look for a Website before they purchase a product or service, even locally! Internet marketing is here to stay. So how can you use this to promote your new (or renewed) brand?

Of course, there are listing sites like VRBO.com. Though you may not be able to post your logo, you can make sure your vacation rental home name is prominent. You can also provide excellent photographs that spotlight your home. Also, you want a profile picture to show you are a real person.

Vacation rental homeowners can also have a Website or blog. Put your logo on them! Use your photographs! And put your logo/photograph on every page, usually the top left is the best placement because it is where the eye is most drawn to when viewing a Webpage.

I am going to list some other Internet marketing strategies. The key is to use your branding consistently and at the right resolution. Why consistently? Because using your brand consistently across marketing mediums ensures that your audience will begin to recognize who you are and what you do! You will gain brand visibility!

Online Marketing Methods

- Vacation Rental Listing Sites
- Website
- Blog

- Social Media: Facebook, Twitter, LinkedIn
- Video Marketing: YouTube, Vimeo
- Article Marketing: Ezinearticles.com
- Forum Marketing
- Email Marketing: Constant Contact, iContact, Get Response
- Pay Per Click: Google, Facebook
- Classified Ads: Craigslist
- Banner Ads
- Ezine Ads
- Teleseminars
- Webinars
- Radio: Blogspot.com
- Podcasts
- Mp3s: iTunes
- iPhones, iPads, Smartphones, Droids

That's a pretty overwhelming list. It's not the purpose of this book to share all the how-tos about all the online methods. That would make a very long book indeed!

I share these online methods with you now so you can start learning. Choose your favorite three or four and master the methods. Know everything about these methods and when you're ready to unveil your brand, you will be ready!

Building a mailing list is a huge online marketing tool. And providing those on your list a free informational product is extremely valuable. One of the offers we gave away was a free report on how to save money for vacations. Would your market want something like that? Who would-n't?

A list is power. A list gives your brand visibility. If you have a regular newsletter with many subscribers, you can expose them again and again to your brand and your vacation rental home. Think about the power of sharing vacation tips and stories to your prospects? They will get to know you and when they are ready to book with a vacation rental, they will call you!

For some Web-building sites, like WordPress, you will need to make a custom banner. This is where image editing software comes in handy. I did this with my blog and online boutique store. I created banners that look the same as the banners on my Website. It was easy to customize with Photoshop and was not too hard to figure out how to insert the proper code into the respective pages.

My vacation rental guru partner, Deborah S. Nelson, created a beautiful WordPress landing page for my home. It reflected the essence of our home perfectly! Just remember to be consistent and make sure your brand is represented well with the right resolution, is readable, and clearly gets across your message, and your brand will get noticed!

## Offline Marketing

Just because Internet marketing is so popular does not mean that traditional marketing is dead. Every business needs a business card. You never know who you are going to run into who will be interested in what you do. You may be in line at the grocery store, working out at your local gym, or attending your son's basketball game. Even your neighbor might be interested in what you have to offer. Perhaps they are having a family reunion and need another house to accommodate all their family members!

You need to look at your whole life as containing several spheres of influence. Remember the television series Six Degrees? The point of the series was to say that basically, we live in a small world. We all know people who know people who know people and we're connected in some way.

Instead of feeling guilty about sharing your business, what if you had a passion for it? Don't you anyway, or why would you be doing it? Why would you even be building a brand? Don't feel like you're trying to sell something. Just share who you are and the excitement you feel about your vacation rental home. Have that 30-second elevator speech handy when people ask about your business. Think about it. It's a common question, "So what do you do?" Have your business card in your wallet or purse, ready to hand out. Just say, "You may or may not be interested, but here's my business card. You can visit my Website if you would like more information.

And by the way, I have a free newsletter full of gold nuggets for vacation ideas." Your business cards, if you follow this book carefully, will not be throwaways. They will be unique. You will want to pass them out because they will be works of art in and of themselves!

What needs to be on your business cards? Your logo, business name, your name, title, Web address, email address, and contact info. On my cards, I have my logo, including my photo, my slogan, my Website address, email, my name and title, and a teaser for my e-zine. My number one goal with these cards is to get people to take action when I hand them out. I want them to go to my Website and sign up for my e-zine. I, obviously, want them to go to my site and make a booking!

Where should you hand out your business cards? The sky's the limit: your local coffee shop's bulletin board, your church, your homeschooling group's freebie table, with your tip at a restaurant, a tradeshow, your local gym—basically, wherever your path takes you, which is your sphere of influence. Perhaps go to your local tourist attractions and find places where you can post your business card. How powerful would that be?

You may want to belong to a vacation rental association. That can elevate the value of your brand in the eyes of your prospects.

### Other Offline Methods

What other kinds of offline marketing methods are available to you? The answer is many! First, you will want to develop your Identity Collateral. What is Identity Collateral? This is the basic printed materials you need to share who you are with prospects. This includes your business cards, stationery, envelopes, thank you cards, and return labels. It also might include brochures, postcards, flyers, and printed newsletters.

Postcards are especially effective for vacation rental homeowners. Why not leave some postcards on your local military base, if the base will give you permission? Perhaps you know of a local convention where future prospects might attend. For instance, here in Colorado Springs, a big venue for vacation rentals is the Air Force Academy graduation. Rentals are booked out a year in advance. How amazing would it be to have postcards at the Academy so that when family members are ready to make a booking, you have already gotten your name out there. My favorite printing company has a mailing service. You can buy a targeted list and have your postcards sent to your market!

A unified look across all these mediums, as well as your online marketing, will build your brand recognition. Why? It exposes viewers to who you are and lets your prospects know you take your business seriously—that you are a professional. That builds your credibility and trustworthiness, which increases your bottom line!

One other offline marketing tool I am going to share with you that has worked well for me is bookmarks. These are inexpensive to print and stand out more than business cards. Plus, they are very useful to a receiver! Make them appealing and your name will be exposed repeatedly!

Another extremely effective offline marketing technique is free CDs or DVDs. I know that Ali Brown, one of my "virtual" mentors, saw a huge increase in lead captures when she used these. Because she must mail the CDs and DVDs to a physical address, she captures those as well as email addresses. Just make sure your branding is consistent, and you will spread your name recognition like wildfire!

What kind of CDs or DVDs could you give out? How about slide shows or movies of your local attractions? Give viewers an insider's view of all the ins and outs of your tourist destination!

Newsletters are an interesting marketing tool. Talk about niche marketing! If you can print and send a newsletter to your target market and if you include gold nuggets of information to help solve their problems—like saving money on vacations—and include a little bit of promotion, you will be getting your name out over and over again. Plus, newsletters are not thrown away as much as other marketing material. If the information is helpful, readers may even share it with their friends or coworkers. This is also very effective online and much cheaper to produce than an actual mailing piece!

But isn't this kind of direct marketing dead? Not necessarily. These days, people get very little physical mail. Mostly junk mail and bills. A newsletter will stand out. They will look twice at it and voila your brand will get noticed.

### Promotional Branded Products

This is where you can get gold out of your logo! What do I mean? I mean that your brand could actually make you money at the same time it is building your name recognition! How? By having your brand made into a promotional branded product! There is an unlimited amount of these kinds of products. There are robes, golf shirts, water bottles, t-shirts, USB drives, coffee mugs, pens, and chocolates, just to name a few.

You can advertise your business on an unlimited amount of products that interest your target market. Now what would happen if you handed these out at a conference? Incredible name recognition! How would your guests feel if you provided promotional products for them? Would that help spread word of mouth about your business? You can also sell these items on your Website and in your home! As your popularity grows, so will the desirability grow for your merchandise!

What's the best source for promotional products? If you want high volume, go with a promotional products consultant. These consultants broker your job with the best factories in the country—and some can outsource out of the country, too! They know how to transform your logo into a product that your prospects will need, want, and desire.

Deborah is a promotional branded products consultant and is an expert in this field. She owns a business called The Adstuff Company. She is going to share in greater detail about this later in the next chapter.

If you want to test out a few products before buying a huge inventory, try CafePress or Zazzle. These sites allow you to design a product directly online. You can upload your artwork and see the product immediately. You can also create a store and drive customers there. Also, CafePress and Zazzle allow personalization. So if you want to sell your logo products "on demand," your clients can personalize the items.

Whatever marketing method you use, remember that it takes several exposures to make a booking. Be consistent and you will build a brand that gets noticed!

### Best Formats

What is the best format and resolution for your logo? I will talk briefly about this here but will have more details in later chapters. This will just give you a general idea:

- Print design: CMYK, TIFF file, 300 dpi
- Web design: RGB or Websafe, JPG or GIF, 72 dpi
- Promotional products: Varies. These companies will tell you what their technical requirements are.

# Your Brand Strategy

Choose three or four methods from online and offline marketing methods and write down how you plan on putting it to effect and the frequency with which you plan on using it.

| ONLINE | Frequency | OFFLINE | Frequency |
|---|---|---|---|
| | | | |

# Assignment

- [ ] 1 Choose three or four online and offline marketing methods and write them in the space provided on page 49. Also include the frequency you plan on doing these activities: daily, weekly, monthly, etc.

# Chapter Six

## Branding with Promotional Products

What are promotional products? Promotional products are items with a logo or custom design imprinted or branded onto the piece. Some great items for the vacation rental business would be postcards, robes, towels, mugs, T-shirts, flash drives, magnets, stickers, and sweatshirts. Think about lightweight, usable and wearable items that won't take up much room in a suitcase for those who are traveling by air.

In order to make promotional products work for you, you will want to develop an incredible logo, and associate the logo with the location of your vacation rental, so your guests will want to buy it to take home and show off the folks back home where they visited! The great thing about this is you can sell these items, get your brand out even further, use the profits to buy new items, and also pay for some of, or your entire, marketing budget.

### Making Money with a Mini-Souvenir Bar

First of all, go easy. Do not invest huge monies in inventory until you discover who your typical vacation rental guest is. This will determine what kind of products will fly out of your mini-store. In order to get good wholesale prices, it will be best to buy a number of similar items in one run.

Embroidery is a great way to start. Once you get an embroidery template (usually costs $50-$100 to set up), you may be able to run a dozen robes, a dozen T-shirts, a dozen hats, and

a dozen tote bags all at once and get a pretty good per piece wholesale price. This way you can see what items are the most popular, and when it's time to reorder, you can bump up the numbers of the more popular items.

Embroidery is also a good option because you won't get charged extra for unlimited colors, as you would in most other printing processes. With traditional silk screening, you will have to pay a set-up charge for each color. Embroidery is higher end, but doesn't necessarily cost more, if you run at least 96 pieces, as well as charge a higher price for them.

You can also order a few hundred pens with your logo and keep those in the home as freebies—just like they do in the hotels. Pens don't cost much more with your logo and name imprinted than they do at an office supply house. You will just need to order at least 250-500 at a time. They will be useful for both you and your guests.

Postcards can be ordered as well, (about $.25 each) and you can sell a batch of 10 postcards for $10. Get some stamps and put them on the postcards. That way, the guest can simply write the postcard from the comfort of the vacation rental and put them in the mailbox without having to go to town and find a post office. Once you get your little branded souvenir corner going, the extra money can pay for your advertising listings—and get your brand out and about as well!

### How to Sell Your Branded Products

I suggest investing in a glass display case. If you buy a used one at a secondhand store you will to keep your investment low. The simplest way to close the sale is to have an order blank with all the products and their prices listed. Use an honors system. (You probably have the guest's credit card number anyway.) Just have them fill out a form, take the products they have bought, and leave the form with a check or credit card information in a box. This is a mini-bar concept. People take the drinks and snacks in the mini bar in a hotel, and expect to get charged for it. Just have clear instructions in your display case: they must fill out the form, and they must leave their check or credit card information on the form.

Secondly, take some nice photos of your promotional items and display them on your website. Let guests know that these items are available for sale at your vacation rental. You can sell them online, too, if you have the patience to do the packing and mailing to ship out the product. I would not recommend this unless you are doing vacation rentals full time and don't mind doing packaging and shipping. I suggest instead you let the impulse shopping mechanism kick in when they are there, and want to take good memories home with them.

Thirdly, include one freebie magnet or postcard packet when they sign their hospitality contract to book a week! Let them know that this is a thank you for booking with your vacation rental brand. Also, on the contract be sure to list additional promotional items with their prices and a check box for purchasing the items. The cost can be added to their deposit or booking fee. You can pre-sell and pre-charge for these items before they come. This is where having photos of the items available on the website can help you add these sales to the bottom line of the booking transaction!

## How to Price Your Promotional Products

You will pay a wholesale price when you purchase the items. If you do your shopping, and if you set up an attractive logo and run many pieces at the same time to get a good variety of products and prices, you can mark up the merchandise double to triple the wholesale price you paid. Over time, this is worth the effort. While it is only a trickle of income that comes from the sale of promotional products, you just might be able to pay your entire advertising and marketing budget with the proceeds as well as give additional branding exposure for free!

## How to Buy Your Promotional Products

There are now places online where you can buy promotional products directly. However, what you are doing is a very specialized idea, and it's best to work with an experienced promotional products specialist who can help you get a wide variety of products in small quantities. It is not wise to carry too much inventory as you may get stuck with products that just don't move. Go slowly and get to know your client base before you buy larger quantities of one item. This is the way to go. This is the way you will get your best pricing. The retail business is tricky, and its best to be conservative until you see what products are actually moving.

Additionally, if you get stuck with a dozen "sleepers," you can offer them to guests for FREE if they agree to go online and fill out your guest book with an authentic positive testimony. That way, you will generate more business with your effort, and not get stuck with too much merchandise that is not very popular.

### The AdStuff Company

The author of this chapter and others in this book, Deborah S. Nelson, has been in the promotional products business for 25 year, and is offering her clients a startup package of 72 pieces of an assortment of souvenir items. It includes one dozen robes, two dozen large and medium t-shirts, one dozen large sweatshirts, one dozen tote bags, one dozen ball caps, for $777 plus shipping and handling. This is based on artwork that is provided in the required digital format. If the artwork provided is not in the required digital format, extra charges will be applied. The retail value of this package is $1,500. Suggested retail for individual items is: robes: $50, (total $600) t-Shirts $10-$240, sweatshirts: $25-$300; caps: $15 ($180) tote bags: $10 each, ($120). Write her at dnelson@theadstuffcompany.com, call 1-888-ADSTUFF (1-237-8833), or go to www.theadstuffcompany.com. This is an unadvertised special for the readers of this book. We hope to hear from you soon.

# Your Promotional Plan

Plan what promotional products you will use to promote your vacation rental brand.

| Promotional Product | Quantity |
| --- | --- |
| | |

# Assignment

- ❑ 1 Choose several promotional products and write them down on Page 55.

- ❑ 2 If you are going to employ the mini-bar idea, start looking for display cases. Craigslist is a very good source for this, but use discretion.

- ❑ 3 Remember to contact Ms. Nelson if you want to take advantage of her special package price for our readers. Write her at dnelson@theadstuffcompany.com, call 1-888-ADSTUFF (1-237-8833), or go to www.theadstuffcompany.com.

# Chapter Seven
## The Best Software to Build Your Vacation Rental Brand

If you want to build a vacation rental brand that gets noticed, these days there's only one way to do it: you must use a computer and design software. But what is the best software? What is the most affordable software? What are some free choices of software that you can use? Also, what equipment do you need? What equipment is essential, what equipment is optional? Keep reading to find out all the info you need to make your brand get noticed!

### Equipment Needed

First of all, let's talk about the equipment you need. Obviously, the most essential piece of equipment is a computer. You want a computer that has enough power to handle a graphics program. You may also want to buy a color printer and scanner. But these items are completely optional. Epson printers are some of the best in the business.

Canon scanners seem to be the best. If you decide on a scanner, you want one with high resolution and the best bit depth. My scanner, the Canon 9950F, has 4800 x 9600 dpi color resolution (max.) and 48-bit color depth for over 281 trillion possible colors. This may be excessive for any scanning you may need to do. Just look around and see what you can find. There are also scanning services available. They possess the best scanners in the graphic arts business, called drum scanners. But for a logo, this kind of scanner may not be needed.

You may want to invest in a digital camera, especially for your vacation rental photographs. Again, Canon makes some of the best cameras on the market. I have been very happy with mine.

## The Best Software

The most professional software, the one I use most for designing logos, is Adobe Photoshop. With Photoshop, you can set your type, make it any color you want, and format it to any type file you can imagine. You can also create curved type, which is an extremely useful ability when designing a logo.

This program's main purpose is to manipulate photos, but it can be used for illustrations as well. It has a lot of flexibility when it comes to manipulating type.

The best software for manipulating or creating illustrations is Adobe Illustrator. Illustrator is complicated, but it is one of the programs used to create promotional products involving silk screening and embroidery. Illustrator files are often called "Vector Art."

I also use QuarkXPress for my printing and design, including the design of this book you are reading. QuarkXPress is a marvelous tool for laying out your identity collateral and marketing materials. It's awkward to use for designing logos, although it can be done. You just have to export it to an EPS and then tweak it in Photoshop. QuarkXPress also has Web capabilities.

Adobe sells the Creative Suite which includes Photoshop, Illustrator, InDesign (comparable to QuarkXPress), Adobe Acrobat Professional, and more. I do not like InDesign as well as QuarkXPress. To me, it's more difficult to understand and not as intuitive. Adobe Acrobat Professional is very handy to have. You can convert any document into PDFs and even make forms. Another option that professionals use is CorelDraw. I have limited experience using this software. PC users are especially drawn to this program.

Where can you buy these programs? First, download their free demos. Most of these companies provide either a 30-day or 60-day trial. You definitely want to "try before you buy." If you decide you want to purchase the software, you might try eBay first. That's how I got my QuarkXPress. Just make sure it's an original not a copy! You do not want pirated software!

Also, if you buy an older version, you will save a lot of money. You may not need the latest and greatest software, especially if you have an older computer. You can also try buying software from Craigslist, but again, watch out! It may be a pirated copy!

## Moderately Priced

The most affordable software for creating logos, hands down, is Photoshop Elements.

If you plan on designing your brand primarily for the Internet, Photoshop Elements is especially helpful. You can design logos, banners, buttons, or whatever else you need to market your vacation rental online.

If you plan on printing marketing materials, Photoshop Elements will limit your choice of vendors. You cannot save files for full-color printing with this software. You might be able to upload files to online printing companies, but your colors will be changed.

I have used Photoshop Elements at times, as it is very user-friendly for photo manipulation software. It worked just fine for creating logos and banners. CorelDraw sells an affordable image editing software called Paintshop Pro. Art software available, if you want to create your own computer graphics, includes Corel Painter, ArtRage, and Corel Painter Essentials. I have had no experience with these software programs so I would suggest searching on Google for reviews.

As far as mid-level page layout software, you might try Microsoft Publisher or Serif PagePlus. Other software includes The Print Shop, Print Artist, and Printmaster, although these are not generally used to develop documents for professional printing.

It's very difficult to design a quality logo using Microsoft products, especially Microsoft Word. Word is particularly hard to control and to manipulate images exactly the way you want them. Brands and marketing materials designed on Word inevitably look amateurish.

You might also find moderately-priced software on Amazon.com. I noticed they had home versions of programs like CorelDraw.

## Free Software

First thing to check if you are looking for free software: what software came with your digital camera or scanner? After searching on Google, I came up with a few free options.

You may want to do some more digging since I already own my graphics software and have had no need until now to find free options!

- **Scribus**—This is reportedly on a par with QuarkXPress and InDesign. You can prepare documents for professional printing with this software. It has a high learning curve. Available for Windows and Mac.
- **OpenOffice.org Productivity Suite**—Said to be better than Microsoft Office. This has a drawing software component.
- **PagePlus Starter Edition**—PagePlus sells advanced editions as well as starter editions. This may be a good place to start if you are a Windows user.
- **PhotoScape**—Great for Window users and has a lot of different options.
- **GIMP for Windows**—Has many features of Adobe Photoshop. Also has a steep learning curve.

Other free options include Paint.net, Serif PhotoPlus, Photo Pos Pro, and Pixia. Free options specifically for the Mac include Seashore, Gimp.app, Inkscape, Scribus, GimpShop, or ImageWell.

Keep in mind that I have not personally tried out these software programs. You can easily do a search for software. Just beware of viruses if you are on Windows! Be sure to check it out for yourself before you download any software programs.

I have also included other software programs I came across that I didn't mention above.

- Software Directory
- Adobe Illustrator
- Adobe PageMaker
- Adobe Photoshop Elements
- Artweave
- CorelDraw
- Corel Painter Essentials
- Gimp.app
- GimpShop
- Adobe Creative Suite
- Adobe InDesign
- Adobe Photoshop
- ArtRage
- Canon
- Corel Painter
- Epson
- GIMP for Windows
- ImageWell

- Inkscape
- Macromedia Freehand
- OpenOffice.org
- Paint.net
- Photo Pos Pro
- Pixia
- Printmaster
- Seashore
- Serif PhotoPlus
- Studio Artist
- WordPerfect
- Macromedia Fireworks
- Microsoft Publisher
- PagePlus Starter Edition
- Paint Shop Pro
- PhotoScape
- Print Artist
- QuarkXPress
- Serif PagePlus
- Scribus
- The Print Shop

# Your Software Choices

I've shared a lot of information about software programs. Now it's your turn to research. In the columns below, write your top three choices for each category after you thoroughly research the programs and what they have to offer.

| PROFESSIONAL | MODERATELY PRICED | FREE |
|---|---|---|
| | | |

# Assignment

- [ ] 1 Research the software program choices I highlighted above. Fill out the form on page 62, writing down your top three choices in each category. Remember that many of the applications that cost money offer a free demo.

- [ ] 2 Decide which program you will use. If it is a paid version, download the demo. If it is a free version, download the software. Now play with it!

# Chapter Eight
## Spark Your Creativity

Where do you find ideas to design your vacation rental brand? Ideas are all around! Just open your eyes and you can spark your creativity!

Being creative is one of my greatest joys! Read on to discover 11 ways that you can get your creative juices flowing. Putting these ideas into practice will help you make a vacation rental brand that gets noticed!

## 11 Ideas to Spark Your Creativity

Creativity. It is an important tool for building a brand that gets noticed! A successful brand cannot be built without it! Creativity can be seen everywhere. Our world is surrounded by creativity. But how can you harness that for building your brand? Read on for 11 ideas that will spark your creativity!

1 **Surround yourself with nature.** God is the most creative being of all. After all, He is the Creator! You can see His creativity in sunsets, in the hues of oceans, in the shape and texture of rocks. Go for a walk and just take in the beauty of God's creation. Stroll on the ocean beach or take a hike on a mountain trail. Nature has given me much inspiration over the years. The color of a sunset became the colors for a design project. The sounds of thunder and rain inspired me to compose a song. Taking time out to enjoy God's creation will refresh your soul and spark your creativity! And it will help you build a brand that gets noticed!

**2 Clear some clutter.** Yes, I know it sounds strange, but doing mundane tasks will actually spark your creativity. Cleaning house, sweeping the floor, and getting rid of junk will clear your mind, dust the cobwebs out of your brain so to speak.

For me, clearing my desk before I work on a creative project is essential. When I start fresh, I feel like the ideas flow better. That sparks creativity!

I once worked on a logo for a gallery in Colorado Springs. Part of my client's philosophy was clearing clutter, so before I designed the logo I swept the kitchen floor. It worked incredibly well! After I finished my task, my mind was as clear as a bell to make an outstanding logo. My client loved it! Clear some clutter in your house or office and your brand will get noticed!

**3 Browse through antique shops or if you like thrift shopping, go look around a store.** Take in the sights of your downtown boutique shops. You don't necessarily have to buy anything, but just looking at all the unique treasures around you will fill your mind with new ideas.

Sometimes these treasures are in your own clothing. Recently I was working on a clay necklace when I happened to look down at my shirt. The flower design gave me an idea. Before that moment, I had no idea what to do. The pattern on my clothing inspired me, sparking my creativity!

Fabrics and textiles are a wonderful source of creativity. I have designed whole brands around fabric! It's easy, fun, inspiring, and unique! Books are another invaluable resource. I get a lot of my ideas from graphic design books by top-notch professionals in the field. I have even taken these with me on a walk, sat on a rock, and poured over the pictures. Ideas came like pools of rain!

Go to your local library or used bookstore. Look on Amazon or surf the Net. Be sure to look at design ideas from the best of the best. But do not copy their work. In order to make it your own and an original, you have to change the idea at LEAST three ways, if not more!

Play tourist for a day in your local area. Go to the museums, amusement parks, fairs, and attractions. Soak up the history and vibrancy of your town. After all, your location is a very important part of your vacation rental brand. Giving your eyes a visual feast will help you make a brand that gets noticed!

4 **Kick up your heels! Have some fun.** Go dancing with your spouse, or go for a bike ride. Watch an inspiring movie. Go skiing or ice skating. Whatever you do, let your little child come out. Enjoy yourself and have a blast. Try new experiences and stretch yourself.

Not long ago, my family and I saw the movie *Soul Surfer* about Bethany Hamilton, the surfer whose arm was bitten off by a shark. This inspiring movie gave me motivation to complete an online course I was working on. If she could overcome her difficulties, then so could I! That movie definitely sparked my creativity! Having fun and being inspired will help you make a brand that gets noticed!

5 **Listen to some music.** When you feed your soul with motivating music, you definitely spark creativity. I personally love soundtracks. *Chronicles of Narnia* and *Lord of the Rings* soundtracks always help me focus, especially when I'm writing or designing. Invariably, I will come up with a new idea that I would not have had otherwise. I am listening to *Lord of the Rings* right now as I write this! Listen to your favorite music and you will spark creativity and your brand will get noticed!

6 **Serendipity.** These are unusual coincidences that are providential in nature.

For instance, recently I made a decision to exercise first thing in the morning, but in order to do that, I knew I needed to buy a new blender to make smoothies since mine had broken. I went to the store to buy one and found that it was marked down to half-price! This gave me even more of a renewed commitment to exercise. And as of this writing, I have been faithful to my commitment.

You might have an idea in your mind and behold, you find the exact piece of artwork you were looking for! Or you decide on a name for your vacation rental business and a close associate or family member has the same brainstorm! Just watch for Providence in your life and you will find incredible sources of creativity that will make your brand get noticed!

7 **Don't be a perfectionist.** This is a huge one. You need to let your inner critic go. Forever. When you sketch something, don't make any judgments. Just sketch! When you are brainstorming business names or slogans, don't think any of them are stupid. Just write them down! Letting go of your inner critic helps you to find that buried creative person underneath! Let your creativity shine through and you will make a brand that gets noticed!

8 **Use your dreams.** What do you dream about? Try to remember. The trick is to review your dream right after you wake up. Keep paper and pen by your bedside to jot down profound dreams. You never know what ideas dreams will spark later on.

Dreams have been an incredible source of creativity for me. I've had some very profound ones. I remember one was so incredible that I got up in the middle of the night and wrote as much as I could remember. Later, I rewrote it and then designed it into an inspirational meditation called "You are a Blooming Original." It's one of my most popular downloads on a homeschooling site on which I am a vendor. Remembering your dreams can be a huge source of creativity and one that helps you build a brand that gets noticed!

9 **Be observant.** Be aware of all your senses. What are the associations that certain smells, sights, textures, or sounds bring? Keep a notebook and jot these down. Go for a drive around town, especially the hot tourist spots. What business signage catches your eye? Branding is all around you! Just giving your eyes this visual feast will help you make a brand that gets noticed! But remember not to plagiarize!

Being observant will help you spark your creativity and then you can make a brand that produces effective results—namely, increased bookings!

**10 Listen.** Do more listening than talking. Ask questions. Remember there are no such things as dumb questions. One of my favorite things to do is people watch. An airport is an especially interesting place to engage in this activity. In *Harriet the Spy*, a children's book by Louise Fitzhugh, the protagonist carries around a notebook and makes observations about everyone around her. While I wouldn't suggest invading people's privacy, being observant of people and dialogue around you can be a very interesting source of creativity and one that can help you make a brand that gets noticed!

**11 Get out of your comfort zone.** Don't let complacency or dull habits bring you down. Find new ways to challenge and stretch yourself!

Last Spring, I decided to make some floral arrangements for an Easter dinner party I hosted. Frankly, I'm scared of making floral arrangements. My brain and my hands just can't seem to agree! Plus, I am intimidated because my mother and sister are very good at floral arranging! But I tried it! I had this marvelous idea while shopping in a thrift store and I made it happen! I let go of my inner critic and just had a blast with it! My guests were delighted and my mother was very impressed!

Try new things, change your routine. Drive a different way to work or school. Shake things up a little. If you do, you will spark your creativity and you will make a brand that gets noticed!

*I hope this gives you some ideas on how you can spark creativity. Creativity is an important ingredient to building a brand that produces effective results!*

# I Will Spark My Creativity By . . .

How will you spark your creativity? Choose your favorite three ideas and write them below. Then go for it!

| Creative Idea #1 | Creative Idea #2 | Creative Idea #3 |
| --- | --- | --- |
| | | |

# Assignment

- ❑ 1 Choose your favorite three creativity ideas. Write them down on page 70. Then go for it!

# Chapter Nine

## Step One to a Vacation Rental Brand that Gets Noticed—Collect Information

Now the real work begins! Discovering your identity is a process, one that requires much analysis and strategic implementation. But don't worry! I am here to guide you through it!

Now we begin our step by step process of building a brand that makes your image gets noticed.

There will be nine steps in all. Some chapters will have more assignments than others.

In this chapter, we will start by analyzing your identity. We will do this in three steps: your **Identity Quest**, your **Visual Quest**, and your **Identity Hunt**. I would suggest writing your responses out in a binder.

You are embarking on an adventure to find your identity and to have it captured visually. In today's business lingo, this is called image branding, which increases consumer awareness about your vacation rental business. The result? Increased bookings!

Finding your identity and creating a logo can be very confusing and difficult to small businesses. Why should you, as a vacation rental homeowner, go through this arduous process? Because if you are serious about growing your business and becoming successful, identity issues need to be thoroughly examined.

How can you discover a new identity, eventually capture it in a logo, and then apply it consistently across all mediums—collateral, literature, signage, Web sites, presentations, and the like? By first collecting information and then performing what's known in the advertising agency world as a Visual Audit. Or as I prefer to call it, in more friendly terms, an Identity Quest.

Collecting as much information as possible about your vacation rental business will result in a full insight into your identity issues and is essential in developing your new brand effectively and efficiently and to your utmost satisfaction.

## Identity Quest

Even if you are not planning on changing your identity (but why would you be reading this book if you are not changing your brand), these questions will help you gain clearer insight into your business and marketing goals, thus bringing you more success. So as you embark on this journey of discovering your new brand identity, answer the following questions thoroughly and thoughtfully and to the best of your knowledge.

If you are starting a new vacation rental business, some of these questions may not apply. Again, just answer to the best of your ability.

Now, ask yourself 20 questions. You can write your responses directly in the book or copy these pages. If you have not created your brand/company yet, then imagine yourself in the vacation rental business. Project yourself into the future, getting a feel for what your business would be like. Some of these questions may seem like duplicates. Answer them anyway. They are designed to draw more and more specific answers out of you. We are essentially drilling down to the bedrock of what your business is. You started this work in the first chapter. Now we are in the process of refining your vision so you can get laser-focus on the best brand for you, a brand that will truly get noticed!

# Identity Quest

1 Why did you (or others) start your vacation rental business and how has it developed?

2 What are your strengths and weaknesses?

3 How do you, as a vacation rental business, treat vendors, customers, employees, neighbors? What is your attitude toward your audience or target market?

4 What is your target market? Who are you in the vacation rental business for? Who is your audience? (Be specific as possible. Even put a picture of your target market on your wall to remind you.)

5 How do employees, vendors, suppliers, neighbors, and the financial community feel about your vacation rental business?

6 Who are your prospects, vendors, and neighbors and how do you interact with them?

7 How do you want your vacation rental business to be seen/perceived? How is it perceived by your audience or your target market?

8 What are the benefits to your customers when a new identity is created for you?

9 Who is your competition, both direct and indirect?

10 What is your vacation rental business vision (refer to Chapter One)?

11 How does your existing graphic identity support your vision?

12 What changes are you trying to affect with this new logo/brand?

13 What are your marketing objectives with this new logo/collateral?

14 Do you have a vision of what the new logo will look like? Feel free to sketch if you like.

15 What do you feel would be a success for this new logo/brand?

16 What are your marketing objectives with this new logo/brand/collateral?

17 How do you direct people/make people aware of your vacation rental business?

18 What is the volume of marketing you want to do with your new brand identity and any new collateral it is applied to?

19 Who are your current designers/suppliers and what are they doing for you/not doing for you? What are your likes/dislikes of the work they are doing for you?

20 What is the single most important point you want to make with a new vacation rental brand identity?

# Visual Quest

If you already have a logo/brand, look at all your Websites, listing sites, marketing collateral, signage, business cards, brochures, video marketing, social media, etc. If you don't have a brand yet, find a business you look up to, preferably someone in the vacation industry. Try to find as much information about them as you can. What does their Website look like, their business cards, brochures, signage... everything you can get your hands on or look at through the Internet? This exercise is also useful to do with your direct and indirect competition.

**Ask Yourself**

1 Is there consistency between all mediums? For example, does the logo on the business card look the same on the Website, signage, social marketing, brochure, etc.?

2 Look at your brand (or the brand you chose to study if you don't have a brand) from a potential client's perspective. Is there any confusion about what your (or their) business offers? Does it encapsulate the essence of your particular Unique Selling Proposition?

3 From the moment a new client steps in your vacation rental home, how is that client treated? How is the client treated on the phone and via the Internet, such as email?

# Identity Hunt

Whether or not you have a brand already, go on a hunt. Collect business cards; observe signage; note Websites you like; look at design books. What kind of style best reflects your vacation rental business? Modern? Traditional? Wild? Conservative? Playful? Bold? Daring? Dependable? Southwest? Victorian? Corporate? Relaxed? Fun? Whimsical? Romantic? Find the word or words that best describe and collect many examples of what you like and don't like. Junk mail is a great source for this research. Don't know where to start? These books are wonderful resources: *Promo2* by Lauri Miller and *Marketing and Promoting Your Work* by Maria Piscopo.

**List your descriptive words below:**

# Assignment

- ❑ 1 Answer the 20 Identity Quest questions.

- ❑ 2 Collect all your collateral (or of a business you admire or compete with) and answer the three Visual Quest questions.

- ❑ 3 Collect as much branding materials as you can, as described in the Identity Hunt section. Keep a file and refer to it often. Even take photographs of different signage and print them out for your reference. Enter in descriptive words that describe your vacation rental business.

# Chapter Ten

## Step Two to a Vacation Rental Brand that Gets Noticed—Name Your Business

"What's in a name?" William Shakespeare wrote in Romeo and Juliet, "That which we call a rose by any other name would smell as sweet." Perhaps, but what would it look like?

Words contain pictures which convey meaning. Your vacation rental business name, if chosen correctly, is the number one clue to what your brand should look like.

If you already have a name, this chapter will:

- Give you confidence that your name is the best,
- Give you guidance that you need to tweak your name a little bit, or,
- Convince you that you need to change your name altogether.

The last option should only be done if absolutely necessary. Renaming a business can be a costly endeavor, especially if you've already built "equity" with your current name!

Remember to use your owner name and photograph on every medium to which you apply your brand. Internet surfers are wary of companies that are faceless. They want to know there's a person behind the business, that it's not just a scam. Plus, in today's social media age, relationship marketing is very important. Come out from behind the curtain and show your vacation rental prospects that you're a real person!

## Generating Ideas

How do you come up with unique business names that fits your identity and makes your brand gets noticed? First of all, you might look at keyword research. What does your target market search for on the Internet? What kind of home are they looking for? An invaluable tool for this is Wordtracker. You can write in keywords like "mountain cabin" and it will give you many variations you would never have thought of on your own.

You can find out how much competition there is for that keyword and how many times per month that keyword is searched for. Once you have determined those keywords, you can create a custom domain name. For instance, a few years ago, Deborah did keyword research for "vacation rental gurus." Through her research, she found out what terms our target market, vacation rental owners, was searching for. We then based our domain name on those keywords. We also used our competitor as a jumping-off point. We wanted our product to sound familiar, yet unique. Our product name was a picture in itself, so it was easy to design a logo for it.

Another invaluable resource I've found for business names is a thesaurus. That's how I came up with my publishing line name, Blooming Originals. I already had an image in mind and what I wanted the message to be. I just looked in the thesaurus until I found the perfect name!

Look back over the questions you've answered in Chapter 1 and Chapter 9. What words are repeated over and over again? Underline or highlight them. Start a list of names. Keep a small notebook with you at all times and when you get an idea, jot it down.

Do a mind map. This method is especially helpful for those of us who are right-brained thinkers. Today there are many software programs to help in this process, especially on iPads.

Once you think you have a name, test it out on people. See what their reaction is.

According to DeNeve, author of *The Designer's Guide to Creating Corporate ID Systems,* business names should be changed only if the business does not convey the true nature of the company, is old-fashioned, difficult to pronounce, or brings up negative associations. Further, she would ask these questions:

- What are the strategic goals of your name, especially if you are re-naming your business?
- What criteria are you looking for?[1]

If you are re-naming your business, what are the strengths and weaknesses of your current name? How will your new name help your business strategy?

## Things to Keep In Mind

What do you need to keep in mind as you create a name for your vacation rental business? In other words, what's in a good name? Well, according to Raleigh Pinskey, author of *101 Ways to Promote Yourself*, a good name:

- Makes your business easy to market.
- Is easy to remember/memorable.
- Simple to pronounce.
- Simple to spell.
- Presents clear understanding of what you do.
- Conveys your target market.
- Stirs interest of prospects.
- Represents you accurately.
- Doesn't confuse you with similar businesses.
- Has a positive ring to it.
- Sounds optimistic.
- Promotes your vacation rental.
- Attracts desired clients.[2]

You want your name to have obvious meaning and a logical tie to the type of vacation rental home you run.

## Choosing Your Name

So, how do you choose the final name? Keep a list and check it twice, of course! Once you have a running list, read through it and ask questions of yourself and trusted people you show it to. I like DeNeve's question. She says average citizens are asked in focus groups for corporate brand names:

- What does this name mean to you?
- What kind of image comes to mind?
- What kind of company does it sound like?
- What kind of products do you think a company with this name might make?[3]

Now, after this analysis, ask yourself and others:

- What is your favorite name?
- Least favorite?
- Why?

Now you should have a few good candidates! What then? Perhaps post the business names on your Facebook page, if you have one. Even hold a contest! Make it fun and exciting!

## Legalities of Your Name

Congratulations! You have a list of good company names in order of preference. So now what? When you get two or three names, the next thing you want to do is check on the legalities of your name. This may not be such an issue with vacation rental homes, but it would be wise to check it out.

You will want to contact the Patent and Trademark Office of the U.S. Department of Commerce. Thankfully, in this Internet age, it's a simple matter of doing a search on the Website to see if your name choice can be used. You are not ready to register your trademark yet. You need to finish your logo before you can do that! So keep reading the lessons and doing your homework and soon you will be ready to file!

You will also want to do a search with your local state department of revenue. If you are just starting your business, you have a few options of legal structure. Two of the most common are a sole proprietorship and limited liability corporation (LLC). At this point, you just want to make sure that no other company is "Doing Business As" (DBA) the same name you plan on Doing Business As.

This step may not be necessary as a vacation rental homeowner. I won't get into the legal particulars here. A good business attorney will steer you in the right direction. If you don't have an attorney, you might want to consider a service like Legal Shield. For less than a cup of coffee per day, you can have access to attorneys, ask them questions, have them review contracts, and much more. My husband and I have found this service to be invaluable, especially when dealing with business questions. Rental properties have numerous tax regulations. Talk to a tax accountant and/or CPA about this. They will know how to handle these issues.

### Register a Domain Name

Once you have decided on a name, you will also want to make sure that the domain name is available. What is a domain name? It's the descriptive URL address of your vacation rental business.

How do you find out if your domain name is available? The best service I've found is GoDaddy.com. You can do a search on their Website and within minutes you will know if your name is available. But watch out for hosting with GoDaddy.com. I've heard that spam filters do not like this service. You may want to register your domain with Hostgator if you need a hosting company, too.

Registering a domain name costs about $12 per year. Even if you don't have your own server for your Website, you can forward your domain name to any Website you choose.

## The Why of Your Name

Answer the questions below about the name you want to choose for your vacation rental business.

- What do you want your name to convey?
- What effect do you want it to have on people?
- What are the strategic goals of your vacation rental business name?
- What criteria do you have for your name?

# Your Name Choices

List the names you have brainstormed for your vacation rental business. Then put them in order of preference.

| FAVORITES | LEAST FAVORITES | WHY? |
| --- | --- | --- |
| | | |

# Narrowing the List Down

Now we are getting down to brass tacks. It's time for you to consolidate your name into your top picks. List your top three choices below and answer the following questions:

*"What does this name mean to you? What kind of image comes to mind? What kind of company does it sound like? What kind of vacation rental home do you think a business with this name might have?"*[4]

1

---

---

---

2

---

---

---

3

---

---

---

# Drum Roll Please: The Final Choice

So now you've done a lot of hard work. You've analyzed, brainstormed, asked trusted friends and associates their opinion. It's time to make a decision. Write down your top choice below:

*"What does this name mean to you? What kind of image comes to mind? What kind of company does it sound like? What kind of vacation rental home do you think a business with this name might have?"*[5]

1 My vacation rental name brand choice:

________________________________________

2 Why I chose it?

________________________________________

3 What is my vision for this vacation rental brand?

________________________________________

4 What are my trusted friends'/associates' opinions of it?

________________________________________

5 Is it available for Trademark registration, DBA registration, and domain registration?

________________________________________

# Assignment

- ☐ 1 Answer the questions on page 90. Start brainstorming a list of possible vacation rental business names. Keep a notebook with you at all times or use a mind-mapping tool. When you have 10–20 names, write them down on page 91 in order of preference and comment why you like or not like the name so much.

- ☐ 2 Narrow your list down to the top three choices. Write these down on page 92. Check with the Trademark office, your department of revenue, and GoDaddy to make sure these names are completely available, if you wish to register them.

- ☐ 3 Decide on your top name and write it down on page 93. Answer the questions.

# Chapter Eleven

## Step Three to a Vacation Rental Brand that Gets Noticed—Write a Slogan

What's the buzz about your vacation rental business? Wouldn't it be great if your business had a buzz? That's why we're going to talk about writing a slogan.

Basically, writing a slogan creates a buzz in your prospects' minds for your vacation rental business. After all, how much buzz have these great slogans created? *"Just Do It."*

*"Because I'm Worth It."* It keeps going and going and going. I 'm certain you can name the brand behind these slogans. Why am I so certain? Because slogans create a buzz in culture. We use them as every day idioms, they become part of our language and we quote them often. So how can you create that buzz for your vacation rental business? Keep reading and find out!

### Why Write a Slogan?

You've worked hard so far on defining your mission, gathering information, and choosing your name. So why would you need a slogan? A slogan makes your name memorable. And when your name is memorable, you will build recognition and brand awareness. And building recognition and brand awareness is not just pie in the sky—it builds trust, credibility, word of mouth advertising, traffic, bookings, and sales!

### What is a Slogan?

A slogan is your mission/vision statement, elevator pitch, and unique selling proposition condensed into a memorable catchphrase. A slogan is a three- to five-word phrase that emphasizes your vacation rental business, giving it a big exclamation point. It's your company motto, a catchphrase, tagline, and mantra. It captures the essence of who you are and what you do in a short, pithy, and memorable statement.

Some slogans are made into jingles, a catchy tune, that makes the slogan even more memorable. Think of the Alka-Seltzer jingle, *"Plop, plop, fizz, fizz, oh what a relief it is!"* I imagine you remember the tune! If you don't, you never saw the commercial. If not, I'm certain you can think of a jingle you do remember! Again, slogans create a buzz. In other words, they get people talking. A really good slogan becomes part of our culture, like Nike's *"Just Do It!"* slogan. Who can forget that one?

A slogan identifies your brand and aids in publicity, promotion, marketing, and advertising. It includes a key benefit to your prospect. What does your potential customer have to gain by staying in your vacation rental home? A good slogan differentiates your vacation rental business from your competitors and is strategic. It describes in a concise way the essence of your business mission/vision and unique selling proposition.

My business slogan is, *"Reach new heights in your life and beyond!"* I use this slogan on my Website, my e-zine, my blog, and my social media profile pages. I use variations of this slogan to communicate my mission.

My slogan is a written description of the picture I use for my logo. That's how I got the idea. In the picture, I am reaching for new heights. To me it is a metaphorical description of my passion of reaching for God's best in my life and my desire to encourage others to do the same.

## How to Write a Slogan

Think of a slogan as a poem. A poem is condensed language that captures the imagination. That's what you need to do in your slogan. Review your company mission/vision/values statements, your unique selling proposition, your 20 Identity Quest questions in Chapter 9. Then, write a 60-second elevator pitch. And what is that? It's the answer to this question: What would you say to a person in an elevator who asks you, *"What do you do?"*

After you write your 60-second elevator speech, make it 30 seconds long, then 10. If you only had 10 seconds, what would you say to prospects to convince them to take a serious look at your business?

You could draw your slogan from keyword research. This would be an effective way to bring traffic to your Website and vacation rental listings. Put the slogan on your listing sites, Website, your blog, your Facebook page, and your article marketing profile page, if you have one, and you will draw more visitors to your business. And these will be targeted visitors based on your keywords. The more visitors you have, the more bookings you will make, especially if they're looking for you! Make sure you use strong action verbs in your slogan. Do not use "to be" verbs, or the passive tense.

Another way to write your slogan is to use alliteration. Alliteration is using the same consonant or vowel at the beginning of each word. This makes the phrase catchy and memorable. Jaguar has a memorable phrase—"Don't Dream It—Drive It!"

You could also use rhyming words. Remember the saying, *"Takes a licking and keeps on ticking?"* Just make sure it's not too corny. Story, metaphors, and similes are other memorable ways to write a slogan, as well as the use of puns or made-up words.

### What Now?

After you write your slogan, your first step is to make sure it isn't trademarked. Check with the Patent and Trademark office just like you did your business name. You do not want legal problems to arise from using a slogan that's already trademarked. This will cost you much money and work. It's not worth it! Once you find out if your slogan is available, you may want to consider trademarking it yourself.

Be sure to check your slogan out with a few trusted associates. Is it memorable? Does it excite them; entice them to find out more about your vacation rental business?

You could literally create a buzz on your Facebook or Twitter accounts by starting a contest. Open it up to your fans, if you have them, and you might get some interesting ideas!

Once you have your slogan, you can use it in vacation rental listing sites, banner ads, embedded links (especially valuable if they are based on keyword research), classified ads, and any marketing materials. You basically have a built-in headline that will draw prospects to view your vacation rental home listings.

# Your 60-Second Elevator Pitch

Write your 60-second elevator pitch below. How would you answer this question if you only had a minute: *"What do you do?"*

# Your 30-Second Elevator Pitch

Write your 30-second elevator pitch below. How would you answer this question if you only had half a minute: *"What do you do?"*

# Your 10-Second Elevator Pitch

Write your 10-second elevator pitch below. How would you answer this question if you only had 10 seconds: *"What do you do?"*

# Keyword Research

Do some research online and find some keywords that you could use for your slogan. Write the best ones below:

# Your Slogan Choices

Write below your final choices for your slogan. Be sure to check that these slogans are available.

| FAVORITES | LEAST FAVORITES | WHY? |
| --- | --- | --- |
| | | |

# Your Top Choice

Now write your top slogan choice below. Congratulations on a job well done!

# Assignment

- [ ] 1 Write your 60-second elevator pitch on page 99. Then on page 100 write your 30-second and 10-second elevator pitch.

- [ ] 2 Do keyword research for your slogan and write your top picks on page 101.

- [ ] 3 On page 102 write some slogans and list them in order of priority. Choose your favorite slogan and write it down on page 103. Be sure that these slogans are not trademarked already.

# Chapter Twelve
## Step Four to a Vacation Rental Brand that Gets Noticed—Develop a Design Strategy

Now we are making some real progress! The more clarity you get on your business, the easier it will be to build a brand that gets noticed! So are you ready to unmask your identity? Great! I'm ready to help!

You have analyzed your mission, vision, values, gifts, talents. You've identified your target market and written your unique selling proposition and consolidated it into a slogan. You've collected your current marketing materials and gathered your favorite examples of brands. Now it's time to review all that data and start to make some decisions about your brand.

Ready to make it get noticed and increase your bookings? Keep reading to find out how! You may be asking, *"Why go through this painstaking process? Why can't I just get that brand now?"* Your goal with building a brand and creating identity is to differentiate yourself from other vacation rental businesses. The key to this? A well-designed logo. It's kind of like cookie-cutter developer houses. If all you have is a mass-produced brand, then it will not be distinguishable from other vacation rental homes. And if your brand is poorly designed, it communicates incompetence to your prospect. It downgrades your trustworthiness and credibility in their eyes.

This chapter will help you form an initial concept of your brand. Then I will break the design development phase into concrete steps. The last step will be to bring it all together into a cohesive design. It takes time to make it right. That's how creativity works. Hastily made logos are not given the time and attention they need.

Remember what I said in the beginning of this course about step-by-step guidelines? The creative process cannot be limited to a specific order. Sometimes the light bulb goes on, triggered by any number of things. I can think of different ways my logo designs came to be conceived. My own company was named after I had selected a picture for my business. I derived the font and colors from a drawing a client gave me. In another case, I mined all the graphics in my computer, drew my own, and combined them into a cohesive whole.

The research phase is an important step to building a brand that gets noticed. Do not skip it to get a pretty logo up. It will do nothing to attract the prospects you want to your vacation rental business.

## Analysis

Review the 20 questions in Chapter 1; 20 questions in Chapter 9; your analysis of existing and naming branding material questions from Chapter 10; and your slogan from Chapter 11. Also look over your file of favorite brands you have collected for Chapter 2.

If you already have a brand identity program, problems will be obvious after a review of the above. Ask yourself:

- Do you see any discrepancies between your goals and the perception of your vacation rental business?
- Is the logo outdated?
- Does your brand adequately reflect your business: who you are and what you do and what kind of home you have?
- If not, what is missing?
- Is it just one element (like your symbol) that needs changing or does it need a complete makeover?

If you discover changes need to be made, then see this as a positive opportunity! I will help you step by step discover your new identity!

So, after you have reviewed all your analysis questions, your current identity materials (if you have any) and your favorite identity brands you've collected, ask yourself, *"What is your ideal identity that you want to achieve?"* Perhaps you want to be cutting edge or bold or convey a sense of reliability, or communicate lasting value. Whatever it is, formulate a statement. I have provided a place at the end of this chapter to do so.

## Successful Strategies

Now that you've reviewed and analyzed all your lesson assignments and materials, it's time to draw some conclusions. After all, we don't want to be guilty of analysis to paralysis!

A successful logo clearly communicates the essence of your vacation rental business. It is unique, not mass produced or overused. A successful logo is memorable and can be easily adapted across all mediums. You may want to consider using your name alone as the logo mark, especially if it doesn't lend itself easily to a graphic identifier. This could be as easy as using your signature. You could also select a typeface and enhance it in different ways as long as it is readable. (I will have a lesson on typography a few chapter farther on, so you can learn all about type then.) You may want to use an illustration or photograph of your home. This would be a logical graphic that would convey what your vacation rental home offers.

Just remember to keep it simple and use aesthetic design principals (I will be sharing in a later chapter about this topic). As a designer I am always on the lookout for unique graphics. Sometimes I sketch these ideas with pen and ink. Other times I bypass that step and go straight to the computer. Other times I Google a phrase and look in the images section. Or, I might turn to my graphics books for inspiration.

Many times I've drawn inspiration from nature—a beautiful sunset or the color of the ocean in the Caribbean. I've found ideas from paintings or even from interior decorating. Fabrics are especially interesting to me. I love the textures and colors I can find in them.

However I pursue an idea, I make sure, in the end, of three criteria:

- Uniqueness
- Originality (not plagiarized!)
- Readability and clarity

# Your Identity Quest

So, now that I've laid a foundation for you, here are the specific decisions you need to make regarding your vacation rental brand. Put a checkmark next to each element you plan to use and then write your criteria for that element below each one.

- ☐ Logo mark or symbol (Photograph, illustration, abstract, computer generated art). Will you even have a logo mark? Consider every possibility!

- ☐ Typefaces

- ☐ Color

- ☐ Paper choices (for marketing materials and identity collateral).

- ☐ Backgrounds (this works well with Website banners, business cards, thank you cards, etc.).

- [ ] Photo of you

- [ ] Other elements and criteria for your brand based on your analysis

This is an overview of all the different elements that go into designing your vacation rental brand. In the next lessons, I will break down these elements into concrete steps.

# Thumbnail Sketches

Now that you are defining your strategic vision, it's time to do some thumbnail sketches! Just have a little creative fun and go for it! You can also make initial designs in your software, print them as thumbnails and paste them here. Then you will be able to evaluate your choices.

# Full Sketch

Now that you've had fun making some initial sketches, print this page out and do a bigger sketch. You can print this out as many times as you want. Or, you can design on software, print it out, and paste here.

# Assignment

- ☐ 1 Analyze and review all the questions you've answered in Chapter 1; 20 questions in Chapter 9; your analysis of existing and name branding material; questions from Chapter 10; and your slogan from Chapter 11. Also look over your file of favorite brands you have collected for Chapter 2.

- ☐ 2 Answer the questions on page 108–109.

- ☐ 3 Make initial concept sketches on pages 110 and 111, either with pencil or on your chosen graphic software and then paste them in the boxes.

# Chapter Thirteen

## Step Five to a Vacation Rental Brand that Gets Noticed—Select a Graphic

Selecting a graphic is a key component to building an effective brand for your vacation rental business. In this chapter, I will be sharing with you how to go about the image selection process and some key resources that will help your brand get noticed! Again, I must remind you about the creative process. It is hard to break it down step by step. But I have chosen the graphic selection first because so often it is the element that determines your color and font choices and more.

You are almost done! You are building a foundation for your vacation rental business that will bring you what you need—a tremendous return on your investment!

Remember that a company's brand is its most valuable asset. As you go through this process, keep that in mind. This is like a treasure hunt! You are going on a quest to find your identity, and that starts with a graphic image!

### Choosing Your Graphic

If you decided as part of your design strategy to use a graphic image, now it is time to select one, whether you prefer a photograph, illustration, or computer artwork.

Since your main selling point is your home, you may want to consider using a photograph of it. Or if you have a descriptive business name, you may want to use a symbolic image.

One of the best sources for graphics I've ever found is Dreamstime.com. They have stunning photographs, incredible illustrations, and best of all, reasonable prices. They usually include a license for using the artwork in logos and identity collateral. In some cases you may have to buy a license if you plan on making them into marketable products besides books.

In Dreamstime and other stock photo sources, you can usually download a free image to play with until you are sure you want to purchase it. These images have a symbol embedded in them that prevents you from using it for your final project, plus the image will be pixilated because they are low resolution. These low-rez images are called "For Position Only" photos in the design world, or FPOs. Sometimes they are called comps.

You will want to credit the artist or photographer. Most stock photo sites explain how to do this.

You will notice in the beginning title page of this book, I have done just that! I used Dreamstime for many projects, including the book cover. First, I searched in Dreamstime for words like "vacation rental" because I knew that was the main thrust of this book on branding. Then I created the cover using the FPOs. When I knew what images I wanted to use in my final file, I purchased the high-resolution JPGs.

You can also find collections of photos, illustrations, clip art, and computer graphics in CD collections. I have often found these at MacWarehouse or MacMall. When choosing clip art, make sure that the graphic is not too "cheesy" or overused. If you use something less than professional or a clichéd, it will reflect on your image!

Be warned—copying something off the Internet to use for your logo is illegal, unless you download a file from a royalty-free site. You need to take your vacation rental business seriously and pay for a license. Otherwise, you will have legal problems as your business expands. Legal problems will cost you much money, time, and aggravation. If you want to be in the business for the long haul, taking shortcuts like this are not worth it!

**Make It Yourself!**

You can use a photo or piece of art you have around the house. I scanned a photo of me as a toddler playing the piano, then using Photoshop to put clouds around it along with a simple frame. The photo represented my aspirations as an artist and the clouds were another tie-in to the angel aspect of my business name. Even with all these design elements, I kept it as simple as possible. This is my AngelArts logo.

I chose a background that I use on all my Websites, business cards, brochures, etc. It is a lace skirt I have! I scanned it in and I use the pattern everywhere. I used lace because lace is a part of my personality. I have been called "The Victorian Queen" by my family members. That's how passionate I am about it. I adore the feminine and I'm not afraid to show it, especially since my audience is mostly women.

I have also designed cards for clients using fabric. For one client, an artist, I scanned her duvet cover material! It encapsulated the wild and fun nature she has as an artist. Then she drew some brushes which I scanned and colored and which complemented the color of the duvet beautifully.

For another client, I scanned one of her favorite shirts! The blue floral pattern fit perfectly with her company name having to do with creativity. I digitally clipped out one section of the material to use as the logo graphic itself. The rest of the material served as a background for business cards, thank you cards, stationery, etc.

One caveat about fabric—make sure it is not licensed—Mickey Mouse, Raggedy Ann and Andy, Beauty and the Beast, etc. Be cautious because even the designs on cloth material is copyrighted!

Another idea I've used with great success is torn construction paper. I decide on the symbol I want, choose some construction paper colors, and glue the design down in layers. Then I scan it and computerize it in Adobe Photoshop and Adobe Illustrator. This makes a very unique logo. In fact, I won a local logo contest using that technique.

If you're good at drawing, you can make a simple drawing and scan it. Use black ink on bright white paper. A heavier weight of paper is best.

If you use a medium other than pen and ink, remember that when using a printing process such as embroidery, you will have to translate these colors into spot colors using a vector program like Adobe Illustrator or Corel Draw. Most likely prepress professionals can help you in this process or they will do the prepress themselves.

For our vacation rental logo, I chose a section of a favorite painting that I had full permission to use. They were Victorian-looking roses. Then I created a romantic looking oval from it. This was the symbol we used for our vacation rental home, called the Victorian Rose. You will want to select a graphic that will work in a variety of ways—on the Web, in print, and on promotional products, as well as full-color process, Web safe colors, and black and white.

Perhaps you are an artist and want to scan in a painting. Perhaps you made a painting or drawing of your vacation rental home! If you don't have a scanner, you can take it to a professional image scanner and have it scanned either on a flat bed scanner, drum scanner, or have a professional digital photograph taken. For the logo, a flat bed scanner would be fine. You don't need as high a quality scan if you were to turn it into a giclée (a high quality ink-jet print). But if you plan on turning your painting into a giclée, and faithful reproduction of color is important to you, drum scanning or digital photography are the best options. Just remember to ask for the digital file! You do not want the scanner or photographer to be the only one with the digitized art because if he goes out of business or moves, you will be out of luck and money!

If you have your own equipment, remember to scan at high resolution. Even 600 dpi is optimal. The bigger the resolution, the bigger the file will be. But you can always make that file smaller. It's much better to go from big to small than small to big!

And if you have an existing photo or illustration and want to make it bigger, you can try to scan it in at maximum resolution. This will in effect "blow up" your original and you might be able to use it. Just make sure it is good quality or your logo will not be well-constructed.

Of course, if you are competent in computer vector art, you can make something yourself in Adobe Illustrator or Corel Draw or other vector program. I have done that many times—like making rays of a sun or creating a simple dove. Also, unless you have a four-color swatch book and your computers are perfectly calibrated, you cannot expect to get the same colors you started with. If you choose spot colors rather than CMYK for 4-color printing, you will want to use a Pantone swatch book. (Refer back to Chapter 4: Essential Elements of a Well-Designed Logo/Brand.) We will talk about color in a later chapter.

### Pay A Professional!

You can also pay an artist, illustrator, or photographer to create your graphic or take a photograph of your home. You should expect to pay them at least $50 an hour. Get a written estimate before you agree to work with them. Most will want to know the parameters of your project, so you need to be ready with all the research you've done up front. If they are good illustrators, artists, or photographers, they will ask you to sign a working agreement or contract. This is to your benefit—you know you are working with a quality person who is trustworthy.

I realize cheap options are out there, like Gurus.com and you can use artists overseas. I cannot personally recommend these places. I did, as a graphic designer sign up for Gurus.com, but as an experienced artist I have never been able to take these jobs seriously. It just isn't worth my time. Most competent designers are going to feel the same way. However, if you do decide to outsource in this way, you are going to be more confident in overseeing the project because you are taking this course and will better understand the design process!

When taking photographs of your home, keep it as simple as possible. Taking the picture from a high angle is best. Get on a ladder or step stool. And do not have any clutter on counters or floors and make sure it is spotless!

### Other Words of Advice

In selecting your graphic, choose something simple and that clearly reflects your business name and USP. Do not confuse your prospects by selecting a graphic that has nothing to do with your business! Remember that a logo graphic isn't so much a Picasso art product, but a symbolic work that serves to communicate a message to your prospect about what makes your company unique. Again, a good photograph of your home would be a good option for your vacation rental business brand.

Keep your logo simple and be sure to do a trademark search so you know your graphic/name combination is not already taken. Ultimately, the trademark is based on both.

### Your Personal Photo

You may at this point start working on getting a good photograph of yourself to use consistently on your business cards, Websites, blogs, and social media accounts. Remember, people want to deal with a real live person, not an unknown entity. You will be calming your prospects' natural fears about committing to an unknown vacation rental.

Before you hire someone, make sure they will give you the rights to use the photograph. You want a photograph that shows the essence of who you are. In other words, since you are a vacation rental owner, you probably don't want to be in a business suit photographed in an office! A natural setting around your home would be best.

Be sure to have good lighting. Flash photography is generally not a good idea because it will wash out your face too much. If professional lighting is not available, have the picture taken outside with the sun behind the camera and shining on your face. Natural lighting will make you look alive. Ideally, you want "catch-light" in your eyes, making them sparkle. This is more attractive and appealing. No light in your eyes will make you look frightening. You do not want to frighten your prospects away!

You want your face to fill two-thirds of the frame. It's people's faces that are appealing. You also don't want any strange objects sticking up behind you! Watch your background and make sure it doesn't clash with what you're wearing. You want to complement the colors you use with your logo, so choose an outfit that coordinates.

Here's an idea that I use for my video backgrounds: buy a simple curtain from a dollar store. Hang this up on a wall in front of a natural light source! Very affordable and convenient, believe me! Or, since you are selling your home's features, choose an attractive setting with plenty of light and take the photograph there.

Remember that you want to create an attractive, appealing photograph. That usually means a nice smile and a warm, inviting look. If your personal photograph is scary looking, you will scare away prospects. If you already have a photograph, make sure that it meets the above criteria before using it in your vacation rental brand.

If you can't afford to pay a professional, have someone you trust take the photograph. Or possibly look for ways to barter or trade services with a photographer. Maybe there's a new photographer out there who is looking to build a portfolio! Craigslist can be a great source for such people, but always be careful with online bulletin boards.

## Technical Aspects

After you make your graphic selection, plan to scan, download, or purchase it in high resolution. You may want to wait to do this after you read Chapter 14 because what you read there might change your mind. That is why an FPO—for placement only—photo is so important!

Ultimately, you need the graphic in at least 300 dpi. Purchasing a TIFF or JPG is preferable and it can be in RGB color. You can change this in image editing software for print design projects, such as your business cards. But until you finalize your design, an FPO is fine. Just make sure you can get your chosen graphic once you make your final selection at a higher resolution.

You want as big a file as possible because you may want to create signs, have business cards printed, or produce brochures. Knowing the output size of a printed piece is essential in this. For instance, for the book cover, I knew I needed artwork at least 8.5 inches wide. You will not lose quality if you scale the graphic down to a lower resolution, like 72 dpi for your Webpage. But if you start with a low resolution object and blow it up, the image will get grainy or dotty when you try to print it at the high resolution that offset or digital printing requires. This is another good reason to avoid copying images off the Internet—they are always low resolution.

And never use a faxed image or an image from something already printed. The saying amongst graphic designers is, "Garbage in, garbage out." If your image is poor quality to begin with, no amount of tweaking is going to make it excellent quality. Start with an excellent image and you will have no worries when it comes to a well-constructed logo.

# Your Selections

Decide which kind of graphic you will use: photograph, illustration (or painting), or computer drawing. Write your choice below:

Where will you find your graphic: a stock photography site like Dreamstime, a collection of images, do it yourself, or hire someone? Write your choice below.

Who is going to do your personal photograph? What setting will it be taken in? What will you be wearing that will coordinate with your color choices (a whole chapter on color is coming, but just remember that whatever you wear needs to complement your logo, not clash with it.) Write your decisions below.

# Your Top Choices

If you like, print out your favorite graphics and paste them below. Sometimes having a birds-eye view of your choices helps you to make better decisions.

# Final Choice

Cut and paste your final selection below.

# Assignment

- [ ] 1 Answer the questions on page 120. Choose the kind of graphic you will use. Then choose the source from which you will select it: a stock photography site, creating it yourself, or hiring it out. Who will do your personal photograph? Plan what you will wear and what setting it will be taken in.

- [ ] 2 Do research and select your graphic. If you decide to do it yourself, do some sketches and decide what your favorite one is. If you want to hire someone, start the process! When you get a few favorite images, cut and paste them if you want to on 121.

- [ ] 3 Before you make your final selection, be sure the image is not trademarked! Download FPOs if you have chosen one from a stock photography site. Scan an image or have it scanned if you have decided to use original art. Get a preliminary sketch from a professional if you choose to hire the graphic out. Select your favorite and if you wish, copy and paste it on page 122.

# Chapter Fourteen
## Step Six to a Vacation Rental Brand that Gets Noticed—Choose Your Colors

Color is such an exciting topic, especially in today's Internet age. Because color is everywhere and it's more affordable than ever in the print design world! Color has meaning and creates a special touch when developing a brand. Maybe I'm a fanatic about color (just step inside my house someday and you'll know just how crazy I am about color), but it makes a huge difference when designing logos, business cards, brochures, or anything!

Choosing color is a very fun and creative process. And yes, there are some technical aspects, too. Colors have meaning and communicate a message. The colors in your logo are especially important because they speak of the essence of your vacation rental business and tell the world what makes your home stand out above the crowd.

In short, colors make sure you get noticed! Colors make you shine! But how do you choose the best colors for your application? What's the most effective use of color? How can you make color appealing to a potential guest? What are the technical aspects of color to keep in mind when designing a logo?

In this chapter, I will share with you all my design secrets about color. The information may get overwhelming at times, but just remember you are receiving a basic overview so you will know the process. This will make you more effective at creating print files or when hiring a graphic designer, if you decide to do so. In turn, knowing design facts will save you much money! In my tenure working with full-color magazines, I became very proficient at the printing process, especially color. I look forward to sharing my knowledge with you!

## Communicating with Color

Seeing a color does something psychologically to our minds. Have you ever noticed how you feel on a dark gloomy day versus a bright sunny day? The infusion of color brightens our mood and the lack of color can sadden us. In a home, a cool color like blue can literally make us feel chilled, while a warm color like burgundy can warm us up. Color affects us emotionally and it greatly affects your potential guests as well.

So how do you make effective color choices? Here's some ideas that will jump start your selection process:

Red

Want to communicate power, excitement, and a cutting-edge dynamic? Is that what describes the personality of your vacation rental business (not just your personality, but the essence of your business?) Then red is a good choice.

Black and Gold, Blue and Silver

Want to have a classy image? A black and gold combination is very elegant. So is blue and silver. But watch out—metallic colors cost extra money! I will explain in a minute.

Is your company inspiring, calming? Blue is a great color!

Orange

Orange connotes urgency—take action immediately!

Purple

Purple expresses royalty and fun. Purple and lime green together is a very playful, fun combination. This is one of my favorite duos of all time. I don't know how many brochures I have designed in these colors. And yes, our playroom/schoolroom is painted in guess what? Lime green and purple! I kid you not! And it works beautifully!

Burgundy

Burgundy or mauve combined with gray is a very straight forward, conservative choice.

Yellow

Yellow is bright and cheery and stimulating—but watch out—it can be very hard to read.

Green

Green is a wonderful color to spread the message of growth, life, development, prosperity, or abundance.

Purple and blue can print much differently than you expect, so be very careful! This is where using Pantone colors is so helpful (more later about that.) In print design, white does not print. It is not actually a color.

You also need to have plenty of what's called white space. You don't want your page or design so cluttered that the audience feels confused. In design, less is more!

It's kind of like poetry. The less words you use, the better. You want to make sure each element has a purpose and a reason for being there. Download a file from a royalty-free site. You need to take your vacation rental business seriously and pay for a license. Otherwise, you will have legal problems as your business expands. Legal problems will cost you much money, time, and aggravation. If you want to be in the business for the long haul, taking shortcuts like this are not worth it!

## Number of Colors

As far as how many colors to use, generally two is a safe answer for the fonts in your brand. But there's no hard and fast rule. You just want to be careful not to use too many colors as that will distract your audience from the message you're trying to get across.

But you also have to remember that a strictly black and white logo may not cut it in today's media-driven world. Face it. You only have seconds to make that first impression on a Webpage or marketing collateral. Make sure the colors stand out without overwhelming the viewer. On the other hand, if you have a really sharp black-and-white image, a black-and-white brand may stand out more than anything else! It will scream, *"This is different,"* because everything else will be in color and your image will be in sharp contrast to that.

### Artistic Ground Rules

Artistically, choosing colors has a few ground rules. You can choose complementary colors or colors that contrast or a combination of both. Complementary colors are colors from the same color family. Like different shades of green. The easiest way to make complementary colors is to choose the darkest color first, say "Reflex Blue," then in your software program screen it down by a percentage. Fifty percent will be a medium blue and 10 percent will be a very light blue. Experiment and see what you like. Or you can choose a green and a blue; or an orange and a red. These are complementary colors, not opposites.

Colors from opposite color families have a contrasting effect. For instance, I told you about my favorite combination, dark purple paired with lime green. This is exciting, vibrant, and fun. When you choose a dark color, say burgundy, if paired with a light color, like light gray, it will give you a superb contrast and will really make your logo stand out. That's what you want it to do—get noticed!

Just be careful not to choose cheesy colors that will look amateurish. For instance, last year I started painting my office yellow and then added red trim. It looked like mustard and ketchup and reminded me of McDonald's! That's not what I wanted my office to be about! Now that example is about painting the walls of the room, but the same thing could easily happen with a logo!

You can also choose a blend for a background or for the lettering of the logo. A blend or gradation is a gradual change from one color to another. For instance, if you want a rainbow effect, you could go from violet to red to yellow to blue to green. Or you can do a blend from a dark shade to a light shade. Software like Photoshop and Illustrator have an unlimited amount of colors you can use! And they make this all automatic! You can do linear, circular, or triangular blends and you can whether the blend is horizontal, vertical, or at an angle.

You may want to choose colors that complement your vacation rental home. If your home has a light, airy feel to it, you may want to reflect that in the colors of your logo. If you use a lot of earth tones, you may want to use earth tones in your logo, too. Or if you have more of a traditional look in your home, you may want to use more pastel colors.

Another thing to keep in mind is that colors have different tones and hues. Photos and art have shadows and highlighting, all of which can be altered in image manipulation software like Photoshop. Some colors are warm, have more of a blue undertone, while some colors are cold, having more of a red overtone.

There are earth colors and there are pastels and then there are primary colors. Just go to your local department store and you will see that most of the home trends have an earth tone. They have more brown in them. Earth tones work great for a modern business. Pastels work great for a traditional company. Primary colors work great for businesses catering to children.

### Print Production

The last thing to remember about colors has to do with print production. When colors touch each other, they trap. Trapping is when .214 inches is cut around a print element to accommodate another print element that is a different color. If the image is simply a reversal, say white type on a black background, it will knockout, or create a hole in the printing plate. The software program will have a tool where you can check the trapping. Most printing companies have a prepress expert who will make sure your document is technically correct.

Remember back in Chapter 4 we talked about different types of colors. For your convenience, I have repeated that section below:

Color—

Computer screens are RGB (Red, Green, Blue)

There are Web safe colors, using Hexadecimal color codes.

Print is done using CMYK ink (Cyan, Magenta, Yellow, Black). It is also called 4-color process or offset printing. This includes most digital color processes, although metal plates are not used for separation of colors, cutting down on the expense for short run printing jobs. You can even add more colors to full color process, such as metallic inks like gold or silver. Don't worry if you don't understand all this. I will cover more about printing processes in a later chapter.

Spot color—One or more colors used in print design, silk screen, or embroidery. Metallic inks can be used for spot color, although this is more expensive. Spot color is seldom used these days because of the convenience and affordability of digital printing. But spot color is used in some promotional products' processes.

Black & white or grayscale—The cheapest printing option but with digital printing color is more affordable than ever. If you want to get noticed, you may want to use color. Although, if you have a striking black and white image, this in itself could make your logo stand out above the crowd!

Now here's some more information you might find helpful:

Printers use what are called color swatch books. The most common one is called Pantone. When I did a lot of print jobs, I used to carefully look at these color swatches and choose them based on the sample strip I had physically in my hands. That way I could tell exactly what color would end up printed. If I was printing in four-color process, I would use a special four-color book that I would refer to where I could find exactly the colors I wanted.

All computer and ink colors are based on percentages. For instance, the color black would be 0% cyan, 0% magenta, 0% yellow, and 100% black. If you wanted to make it purple, you would make a percentage of cyan and magenta.

It is very similar to combining primary paint colors. What do you get when you mix blue and yellow? Green, of course!

You can actually access these swatch books in most desktop publishing and image manipulation software. It is usually under a "colors" tab. You can create your own colors or choose a Pantone swatch.

Colors will change depending on the medium you use, especially print. On top of the color, a glossy or matte coat may be applied. If it is applied it is called coated. If it is not applied, it is uncoated. Glossy coating is best for photographs while matte is best for artistic works.

Image manipulation software uses a basic unit for colors called a pixel. If you enlarge the window of a Photoshop file to its maximum zoom, you will discover that the image is made up of little squares. These are the pixels that I'm talking about. These pixels translate to dots, as they are calling in the printing world. Each image, including text, is made up of tiny dots. How a dot will behave when printed depends on the color, weight, and texture of the paper. For instance, a dot will spread out more on a rough type of paper. Recently, I tried printing a watercolor art card on cotton paper. The effect was beautiful! The dots spread all over the paper, creating an unforgettable effect! But that wouldn't be good if you are trying to reproduce a photograph and want it to be crisp and clear. In that case, a glossy heavyweight paper would be best.

Colors will also be affected by the color of the paper itself. It can change the whole look of the design. One of my favorite papers to use is a speckle-toned beige paper. This creates a striking effect, especially if the design is black and white.

Inkjet printers also use process inks. My Epson Stylus R2400 uses several shades of cyan, magenta, yellow, and black. You can find high-resolution paper that will show off your work very well. A good inkjet printer is something very handy to have. Not only can you print your logo and see it on paper, you can design and print letterhead, labels, envelopes, brochures, flyers, thank you cards, signs, you name it.

I do not, however, recommend printing business cards on inkjets, at least not for the long-term. I have my business cards printed at a digital printer (I will tell you more about them in my last lesson) and all my other materials printed using my inkjets.

When choosing colors, it is a very important consideration to think about pricing for your printed materials. With digital printing, full-color design projects are more affordable than ever, in fact much cheaper and easier than traditional offset printing. And even offset printing has turned digital in that the plates are made through the computer rather than through film, as used to be the case.

For brand identity systems, Pantone matching systems are used frequently. For instance, your logo text may always be printed in Pantone 2685 M. That is the standard. But with digital printing and Web design, this is not so much an issue anymore. Of course, with the Internet, the color of paper isn't so much an issue, either. But you still have to be aware of background color. There are so many choices available these days. Do keep in mind that white type on a dark background is not as readable as the other way around.

It's best to have several boxes if you want a striking color play. For example, on my Brand Identity Mentor blog, I have a light yellow background, chosen to complement the yellow in my banner. I have the dark banner with my blog name reversed out. In the text, I use black and a dark orange that complements the banner color. The type is on top of a white background for maximum readability.

If you want to choose a spot color, you need to set that up in a vector program like Illustrator or design software like QuarkXPress. In QuarkXPress, click the spot color box.

There is also something called screen angles. This determines the angle that the shades of a spot color will be printed. Generally, you want the same halftone settings as the process color you select when printing the document. Even the spot colors are based on percentages. So if you take one of the Pantone colors and switch it to CMYK in the color dialogue box, you can find out what's the highest percentage. Make that the screen angle. For instance, say you chose Pantone 2685 N. When you open it in the color box, you change it to CMYK and discover that it is 92% cyan, 100% magenta, 0% yellow, and 10% black. You will want to set the halftone angle at process cyan since it has the most percentage.

Just a word about printing in black: to get the truest color, be sure to build it in 100% black like I mentioned before: 0% Cyan, 0% Magenta, 0% Yellow, 100% Black. A handy naming system for color process is to name it like this: 100c, 100m, 0y, 0k. That would be purple. The main colors are already named for you. Or, you can just name it something descriptive and memorable.

Colors on your computer screen will not look the same as the original digital file, scan, or printed version. Unless you have sophisticated color matching software, you cannot rely on the color you see on your screen. That is why a Pantone swatch book is so important. If color integrity is important to you, you will want to look at a Pantone swatch in natural lighting to get a feel for exactly how that color will turn out.

Overwhelmed with the technical detail? No worries! Most print companies have professional prepress operators. They will prepare your document. But just realize, the more technically correct your file is, the better your print job will go and the more you will save time and money. Technical errors can cost you a boatload of money, so if you are not sure, it is best to talk to a technical specifications expert before you even design the project!

### Other Ways to Choose Colors

Here are some handy ways to choose colors that I use all the time. This will help you in your selection process.

If you have an image selected from Chapter 11, open it up in a photo manipulation software program like Photoshop. Select the eye-dropper tool. Now click on the color on the image that appeals to you (see figure 1). Click on the color box located near the bottom of the tool box. This box will be the same color that you selected with the eye-dropper tool (see figure 2).

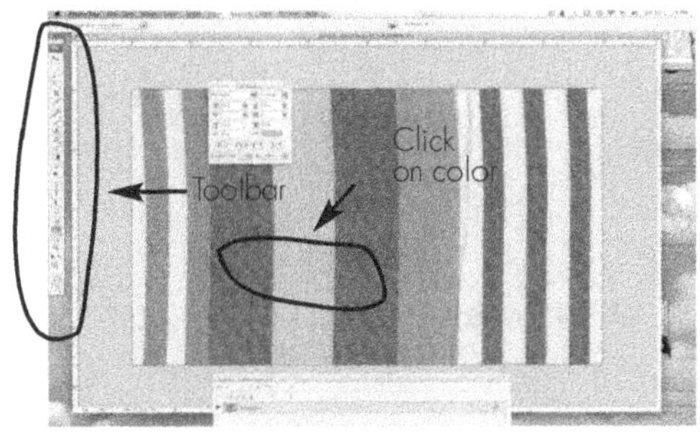


**Figure 1**

Notice the percentage of colors in the window. There is a different one for RGB and CMYK. If you want Web-safe colors, click the box ("Only Web Colors"). Now you know what the exact percentage is for all three—RGB, CMYK, and Web safe. You can always be consistent using this method.

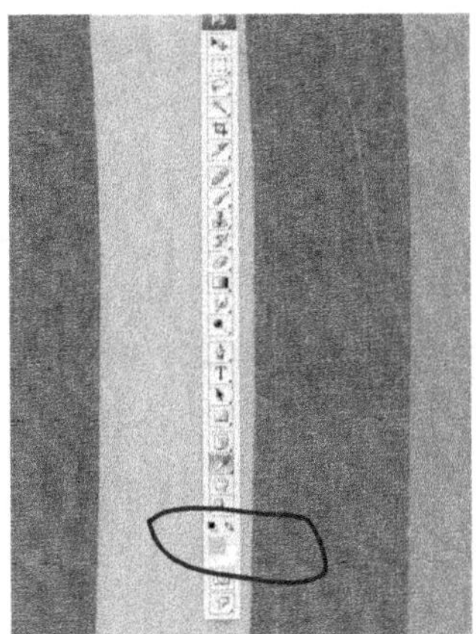

**Figure 2**

Where do you use these colors? Use them in your font selections for your vacation rental business name (we will be discussing font

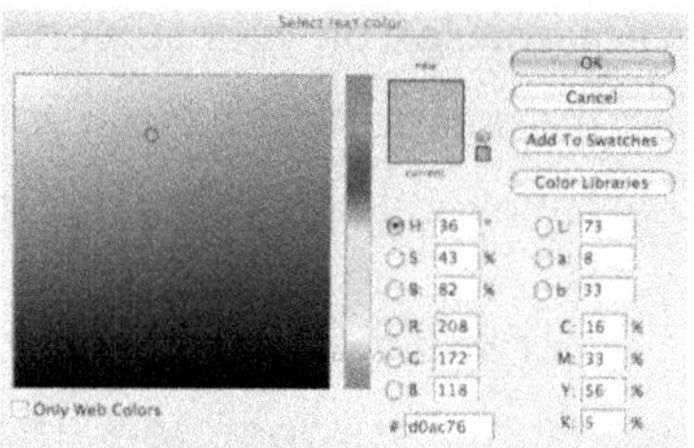


**Figure 3**

choices next). Use these colors to choose backgrounds for your blogs, for your business cards, or your Website.

Here's another idea I came up with while I was writing this lesson: Google the color you are interested in and then click image. You will get some very interesting color and background ideas. Just remember this is for information purposes only! Use this as a springboard to creativity. Do not steal artwork! You could also search for a specific color in Dreamstime.com. Then you can purchase the artwork and you will be good to go.

I already mentioned fabric to help you make color selections. The beautiful thing about software is you can scan something in and then tweak the color to your liking, making it work for your image as well as the background! You scan in RGB mode and then change it to CMYK for print projects. That is how I got the color for my AngelArts logo. I scanned in my lace skirt and played with it until I got the color I wanted. Then I used the eyedropper tool to find out exactly what color it was. I used that for my logo design. I also found a close approximation for Web safe colors. Now all the colors are uniform in my business card, Website, e-zine, and blog!

### One Last Word

As you can see, color is a big subject! I could write endlessly on this topic but I don't want to bore you with too many details! Here is the bottom line: choose colors that will enhance your message, complement your chosen image, and work in a variety of mediums.

Make sure your logo looks just as good on a black and white book as on an embroidered cap. As good on a business card as on a Website. It needs to be the same quality in grayscale, RGB, CMYK, and spot color mode. This will require you have different versions of your logo. We will cover this topic in an upcoming chapter.

# Your Selections

Decide what your color choices are by answering the following:

The mood I want to invoke is:

______________________________________________________________________

I will choose the color by this method:

______________________________________________________________________

These are the colors I've chosen:

______________________________________________________________________

The percentage of these colors are:

______________________________________________________________________

RGB:
CMYK:
Spot: Pantone ______
Web safe: #_______

RGB:
CMYK:
Spot: Pantone ______
Web safe: #_______

RGB:
CMYK:
Spot: Pantone ______
Web safe: #_______

# Assignment

❑ 1 Answer the questions on page 135. Decide what mood you want to communicate with color. Figure out how you will find that color, whether through a Pantone swatch book or by directly clicking on the image you selected. Break down the percentages of the colors in RGB, CMYK, spot (if desired) and Web safe colors.

# Chapter Fifteen

## Step Seven to a Vacation Rental Brand that Gets Noticed—Select Your Fonts

Fonts are the crucial component of developing a vacation rental brand that gets noticed. And it happens to be one of my favorite subjects. I can't wait to share with you how fonts can propel your vacation rental business to new heights! Selecting a font can make or break your logo design. There are certain rules you need to be aware of. You need to know when you can break these rules to express your creative license!

Typography is a whole art in itself. It takes finesse, thoughtfulness, and creativity. Your use of typography can set you apart as a vacation rental business owner. Apply this chapter well and your brand will sizzle! Back in the day of moveable type, fontography was a painstaking process. But the selection of the type is what sets one logo apart from another.

These days, of course, fonts are available to anyone. However, the advent of computers has also brought the deterioration of typesetting standards. Most people who rely on cheap logo design services have no idea what these standards are. By learning about these standards and about typography, you will be setting yourself apart from the crowd. You will truly come across as a professional vacation rental business that takes service seriously. When you take your brand seriously, your prospects notice and this builds trust and credibility. This will result in more bookings. That's why this step is so crucial. The fonts you choose will make or break your logo!

As in everything that has to do with logo design, simplicity is key. It's easy to get excited about making fonts fancy with drop shadows, embossing, gradients, and patterns, but it can be excessive. Remember, you want your message to be communicated effectively and immediately.

Plus, these fonts need to look good in print form. Before you make the final selection, you may want to print them on your printer and see what they look like on paper.

### Words are Pictures

Think of your vacation rental name as a word picture. Close your eyes and imagine an illustration that goes with each word. Words have connotations as well as definitions. They have associations. Have you ever played one of those association word games?

What are these connotations? And how do you find them? Keep reading and I will explain in this chapter through plenty of instruction and examples.

First, let's finish the initial exercise. Think about each word in your vacation rental identity name. Do you have a word picture? How would you describe that word? Write it down! (There is a place at the end of the chapter to record your findings.)

Now you need to go on a hunt for your fonts!

### Font Basics

Generally, you want two different kinds of font typefaces. This rule can be broken, but if you break it, make sure the message is getting through. As I've shared before, there are three different types of fonts:

- *Decorative*
- **Sans serif**
- Serif

Decorative fonts are extremely specialized and usually only used for headlines. These are useful for logos, if they are readable. If more than two fonts are desired, a decorative font is a good choice.

A serif font has lines on the edges of the type. There are many different kinds of serif fonts. Many of them are classic and have a traditional feel to them. Sans serif fonts do not have the lines on them. These fonts are plain. A sans serif font sometimes looks more modern. Again, make sure the font is readable, especially if you plan to use it in large body of text.

Choose a combination of these fonts that is appealing to the eye, contrasts with each other (serif and sans serif together is a great contrast), and communicates the meaning—the word picture—of your vacation rental business name. As you choose fonts you will want to use one font for large bodies of text: copy for an ad, book, brochure, newsletter, or Website. (This is harder to match, but do the best you can. There are a limited number of fonts you can use for the Internet). These need to be consistent with your brand, too! With some computer software, you are not limited to a vertical or horizontal line. You can make your words straight, wavy, a flag, an arc, distorted, at an angle, and others. You can also give them shadows, emboss them, blend them, put a pattern on them or gradient on them. Use caps sparingly. All caps are hard to read, and excessive caps in body copy actually detract from your message. It makes the text harder to read.

Just a note about typing in general for brochures, newsletters, ads, and etc. Many of you were taught in your typing classes to have two spaces after the end of a sentence. This is wrong for typography design. You only need one space!

Choose your font colors carefully to complement the graphic you chose. Again, simplicity and readability are the key factors when making your choices. You will also most likely want to use different sizes of fonts. What is the most important word in your logo? Make it the biggest, make it a different color, or make it bold or italic.

Fonts are licensed, so make sure you have permission to use them. Your computer has limited fonts. Macs have a decent selection. You can buy font collections at various places like Apple.com, CDW.com, and even OfficeDepot.com. More advanced collections from places like Adobe can be expensive, but the type choices are very professional. Remember you want your slogan to be set in a matching font as well!

## The Importance of Typography

Typography is important for three reasons:.

- It makes type readable for an audience. This is incredibly important in print design. If no one can read a printed piece than it is a failure!
- It distinguishes the piece as something that is professional, as opposed to amateurish.
- Words convey meanings and therefore, type is a very important element in design to assist in communicating a message and to call to action.

Typography is the art of using fonts in different ways to communicate a message and aid in the readability of a printed piece. It includes important symbols to assist in effective communication. Typography also needs to be consistent. When setting type, especially for a document, it is important to remember to have consistent spaces for margins and between headings. Nothing speaks amateur hour more than a document that has varying amounts of distance between a headline and body copy. Also, if you decide to capitalize all words in a headline, capitalize the words in every headline! I can't emphasize enough how important it is to be consistent!

## The Rules of Typography

Typically a logo should have no more than two fonts, usually one serif and one sans serif. Or one serif and one decorative. Or one sans serif and the other decorative. This rule, however, can be broken by an astute designer.

Consistency in using these fonts is key to a successful design. You need to use them on your business cards, postcards, brochures, Website banners, signage, etc. So be sure you are happy with the fonts you select and that they have great versatility. You also want to make sure your fonts will look good in black and white as well as whatever colors you choose.

You probably know that fonts are sized using points. Typically in a brochure or newsletter 10 point type is standard for the body copy. In a blog or a Website, a larger type face, even as large as 16 point, has been proven to be more readable for viewers.

Here are some other elements of typography:

- **Leading**—the space between lines of type.
- **Kerning**—the space between letters.
- **Scale**—squeezing or expanding a font horizontally or vertically.
- **Drop caps**—a larger letter that spans several lines.
- **Indenting**—the first line of a paragraph is moved over from the left margin.
- **Baseline**—the line on the art board to which type is locked to create uniformity in columns.

These typography elements don't matter so much when it comes to your vacation rental logo design, but when you start designing identity collateral and marketing materials, it is definitely something to be aware of. And the more awareness you have about typography, the more professional your printed pieces are going to look.

Here is some important information you need to know to make sure your piece is professional:

- **Leading**—leading is the space between lines. In page layout programs, this can be altered to a very precise degree. This preciseness can't be achieved through line spacing found in word processing programs.
- **Kerning**—kerning is adjusting space between letters, usually to make them overlap.
- **Scale**—type can be applied either horizontally or vertically so that the words are made smaller or larger while squeezing or expanding.
- **Drop caps**—large initial letters that draw the reader into the copy. Drop caps have been proven to increase readership.
- **Indenting**—starting the first line of text further into the page in a paragraph, leaving a space. In typesetting, the normal amount of space is three spaces from the left margin.
- **Baseline**—the grid that is on the document or art board, based on a fixed amount of leading made in the preferences section of the page layout program.

Here are some more ways to make sure your piece is professional:

### Smart Quotes vs. Inch Marks

To me text *screams* amateur when inch or foot marks are used in print design. For example: "vs." and 'vs.' Most programs have a selection "Use Smart Quotes" in the preferences menu. But watch out, these do not translate in Web pages, except as PDFs.

### Em dashes

An Em dash is used in a sentence with a dash: "My dog ate my homework—and my cat did, too!" It is made on the Mac by pressing the shift+option+dash key. You will need to do some research on Windows PCs to find the key strokes.

### En dashes

An En dash is used when substituting the word "through" 4 PM – 5 PM. This is made on the Mac by pressing the option+dash key. These also do not translate on the Internet. You will have to use plain old ordinary double dashes.

### Ellipses

Ellipses are the dots used in sentences, My cats got their shots today...and boy, were they mad! This is made in the Mac by pressing the option+colon key.

### Bold Face

Bold face and the use of different colors to aid in readability. Using bold face and colors to highlight key ideas and to lessen gray areas of text is a very effective way to increase readability of a piece.

### Paragraphs

Paragraphs—should not be long. Long paragraphs can overwhelm your audience and could lead them to stop reading your piece.

### ALL CAPS vs. Small Caps

ALL CAPS are hard to read and can look amateurish if overdone. Use sparingly.

SMALL CAPS are easier to read and this is normally a better choice. Used in AM and PM so it looks like this: AM and PM. SMALL CAPS are much easier to read than ALL CAPS!

## The Creativity of Fonts

Now that you know some of the technical aspects of typography, let's talk about the fun part—words as pictures. If you think through this, you will find your creativity in design greatly expanded. If you begin to see words as word pictures, you will find your creativity in design greatly expanded.

Ask these questions:

- What is the connotation of the word?
- What kind of movement does the word have?
- What does the word mean?
- What kind of play on words does it have?

In programs like Adobe Photoshop, you can do curved type. You can also do this in Quark with a special extension. I find it very easy in Photoshop. I often design logos in this program.

Let's look at some examples of logos I have designed.

"Dreams" needed to have an ethereal effect to it, thus I chose a script font (decorative) and curved it to make it float. The "to" needed to be neutral, so I chose a sans serif, which is also used in the body copy of the book I designed. The "reality" needed to be stark and down to earth and contrast with "Dreams," so I chose this outline font. Now here's an example of using three fonts, but it is consistently applied throughout the book for which it was designed! (Which was written by Deborah, by the way!)

I wanted the "Blooming" to grow, so I made it arc up. I also created solid colors in the top and shaded colors in the bottom. Eventually I want to replace the roses with a hand-drawing to represent a rose in full bloom with buds surrounding it. I also think it would be kind of interesting to have a calligrapher do the lettering. Then the art would be all original and would reflect the name better.

Here I wanted the "brushes" to be the most important part of the logo, to highlight the fact that Ann is an artist. I made "Ann" very simple to contrast with "Brushes" which is a decorative font reminiscent of a paintbrush. I incorporated the illustration with the letter "B."

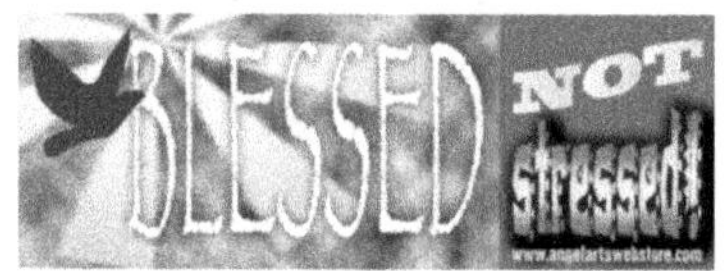


In this example, I made "blessed" light and airy. The dove is incorporated with the "B." The "NOT" is decorative. I chose it to make the word stand out. I capitalized it because it needed that kind of evenness in the design. I made it go up to emphasize the word. Then I made "stressed" very hot and distressed and put fire in it!

With the WaveFront Sciences logo, I created a design that went with the graphic, an actual wavefront sensor my client had made into art. The "WaveFront" is more fancy to go with the word. Science is plain, in a sans serif.

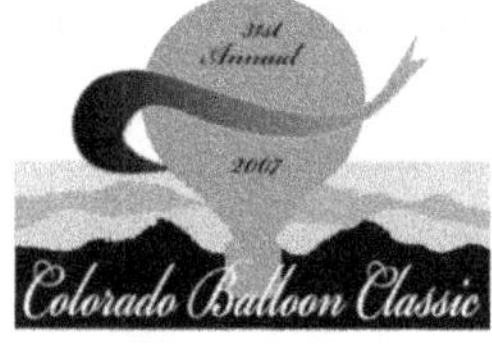


Here's an example of a very simple font selection. I just chose one. And this font was a calligraphy style to go along with the idea of "classic." The client liked it very much considering I won the logo contest that year and I got to ride in a balloon as my prize!

With this logo, I chose "Creative" to have a lot of flourish and to reflect the personality of my client. The "Works" was set in a sans serif to make the logo have contrast.

For this conference logo, I made the "God's Healing Power" simple and gave the "for the NOW!" some punch by using a quirky font.

For The Colorado Collection logo, I shaped Colorado around the oval in a font that reminded me of the West but wasn't overdone. "The" and "Collection" were set in a sans serif and placed in a wave fashion using Photoshop.

Some of these logos took 15 minutes while others took hours. But when all the principles of typography are kept in mind, conceiving a logo or type scheme doesn't take long. Of course, this speed develops with practice and experience.

## How Is Typography Done?

So I've explained to you the why and what about typography. Now let me talk a little bit about how. To do that, I will need to demonstrate an actual design. For this example, I will choose Photoshop. These instructions are useful when you have a document already opened. Remember you want to design in a large format and then scale down. I like to start with a file that's 10 inches by 10 inches at 300 dpi.

1) To select a font, click on the Text tool. Its symbol is a "T" for text.

2) Click somewhere on your document. Type your word or words. To change the font, you can select all and then choose your font from the drop down menu on the top, below the menus.

3) On the row, you can choose size, justification (centered, left justified, etc.), color, curved text—if desired, and paragraph and character settings. If you like your changes, you click the checkmark. If you don't like it, you click the "no" symbol—the circle with the line through it. When you click on the document with the Text tool, it's going to automatically make a new layer for you. That is how Photoshop is built, in layers. You can click on your word with the Text tool and then it will become editable.

If you want your text to curve, choose the curve tool from the font row. Click on the text curve symbol and you can make it an arc, flag, wave, and much more. You can choose what direction to curve in to put in an arc. You can decide how distorted you want it, and if you want it horizontal or vertical.

To change paragraph and character settings, click on the paragraph symbol while editing the type. It is right after the curve text tool. In this window, you have two tabs: character and paragraph. You can change all the character settings in the first tab, including font, smoothness, leading, kerning, color and style, like superscript, bold, italic, underline, etc.

On the paragraph tab, you can choose your desired justification as well as indentation settings. You can decide whether or not you want to hyphenate by clicking or unclicking the box. You can also add space before and after the paragraphs. When designing a logo, I suggest using several layers of text. That way you can move each word around separately.

To move each word layer, click on the first tool, the Move tool. Just move your mouse around to place it where you want it. If you want a different layer style for your word or words, go to Layer/Layer Style. Click on your desired outcome, like drop shadow, bevel and emboss, and inner shadow. This is where you will find the gradient setting for text, too. There are many settings here. It would take a complete new course to teach Photoshop to you, so the bottom line is, just play with it. Don't be afraid!

Now one final technical word before I close this chapter: When designing fonts, you need the font file that goes with that font. You need the font file, sometimes a TrueType file, sometimes a Postscript file, loaded in the appropriate folder. For Macs, that folder is the Fonts folder which is in the Library folder.

When you print your logo or any other document, you need to make sure you have that font in your computer. If you give the layout file to a professional without making it a PDF, TIFF, or JPG, you will need to give them the fonts, too. If you convert the fonts to outlines in Illustrator or Photoshop, you don't have to worry about sending the fonts. This is called rasterizing.

Also, to make a job print correctly you need the style fonts, too. You need a file for each style, like bold, italic, black, etc. Select the specific font in your computer document. Don't press the Bold or Italic button. You only have to worry about this for print jobs.

Generally, you will want to use Postscript font for printing, OpenType fonts for fine typography, and TrueType if you will only be using a font for screen viewing.

# Your Selections

Decide what your font choices are by answering the following:

What is the connotation of my words?

---

What kind of movement do the words have?

---

What kind of play on words does it have?

---

My serif choice:

---

My sans serif choice:

---

My decorative font choice:

---

# Assignment

☐ 1 Answer the questions on page 148. Imagine what your words look like. See them in a picture. Go exploring in an image manipulation program like Photoshop and choose up to two fonts that capture the essence of your vacation rental brand identity. If you are really brave, you can choose up to three.

# Chapter Sixteen

## Step Eight to a Vacation Rental Brand that Gets Noticed—Put It All Together!

Now is when it all comes together. You will see tangible results and have something you can be proud of. That's why I love graphic design. Visuals provide an immediate accomplishment that is truly satisfying. This graphic is like a new beginning. Revel in your accomplishment of completing these steps in a diligent manner.

After you complete this chapter, you can practice this process over and over again until it's second nature. You can take the principles learned and apply them to any number of brands and projects. This chapter will be like a mini-graphic design tutorial.

I will take one of the logos I designed and show you step by step how it's done. I will use one of the most popular image manipulation programs out there—Adobe Photoshop.

If you haven't done so already, you need to download or purchase software for your designs. Refer back to the chapter on software. This is a thorough guide that will help you make the best decision for you and your budget.

Photoshop Elements is an excellent choice if you are going to do mainly Web graphics and want a lower-priced program. What I love about it is you can easily make banners and animated buttons.

You might also refer back to Chapter 4 that gave you an overview of design elements. Have fun in the process and remember that creativity is the biggest component of all!

**What's Next?**

Now that you've chosen your graphic, overall color scheme, and font, it's time to bring it all together. The first question to ask yourself is: What is the most important component? What do you want your target market to notice first? Second? Third?

I actually make a list, starting with the most important one. If it's the graphic, then make the graphic the biggest element in your logo. Next, size the other elements according to your priorities. If it's a word in your name, you don't necessarily have to make it the biggest component, but you might make it more noticeable by bolding it or making it a strong color. This is the element of "weight" that I was referring to in Chapter 4. Remember you have only seconds to get your impressions across! Don't waste those seconds by making unimportant components the most prominent one in your logo.

Now that you have all the components chosen, it's time to design! Sketching by hand is the old-fashioned way of rendering a concept. If this suits you, then do it. If you want to expand on the sketches you've already done in the previous chapters, then do so. Just don't get stuck in analysis to paralysis. After all, the sketch doesn't have to be perfect—it's just a road map to guide you in designing the logo. Think of your whole image as a shape. Usually rectangles work best, but circles are also very effective. Now you want to size your image according to the importance you gave it earlier. Place your image in the desired size and move it until it's artistically appealing. In other words, the graphic is lined up vertically and horizontally with the fonts. Actually drawing a box or circle around your logo will help a great deal. Or use guide marks. Also, zooming in on your logo really helps you get it exact.

What do I mean by lined up? Make sure the edges of the graphic line up/touch exactly with some other elements of your type or graphic. Do I mean centered? No. Actually asymmetrical logos look more professional then centered ones. For instance, I'm looking at a typeface right now on a book: Tarzan of the Apes. "Tarzan" is in red in big block letters, "of the apes" is smaller, left justified, blue, and spaced a little way from the "N" but set at a 90 degree angle. The top of the letters of "O" line up with the top of the letter "N" of Tarzan. The bottom of "Apes" lines up with the bottom of "N."

## Your Tutorial

Since graphic design is visual, I am now going to give you a step-by-step example of the mechanics of design. I will do this by recreating one of the logos that I have designed in the past. You might want to follow along in Photoshop or whatever program you have. If you have something other than Photoshop or it is PC based, you will have to do some research on your own. But this tutorial will give you an overview of how to bring all your previous decisions into a finished product. As you become more comfortable in the process, these steps do not have to be taken in any certain order.

Draw the illustration on heavy-duty, bright-white paper. Pen is best, but pencil will work, too. In this example, my client used a pencil to make the paintbrushes. If you are choosing an image from a stock photo site, download a For Position Only or high resolution image if you are sure you will be using it. If you are using your own image, scan it in. You might want to scan it in at 600 dpi or larger, just to make sure it's crisp and clear and you have greater flexibility with output. If you are using a background, also scan it, download it, or copy it onto your desktop.

For the example of Ann's Brushes, my client decided to use this material that I scanned in. It reflected her artistic nature and personality. Again, scan it or buy it at a higher resolution.

Choose your colors, as I described in Chapter 14. For this logo, I directly clicked on the deep burgundy and the green using the eyedropper tool in Photoshop. For this logo, I chose these two colors. Alter the colors in the illustration if you need to. With the Ann's Brushes logo, I selected each paintbrush with the magic wand tool and replaced the colors with the burgundy and green selected from the material. I made the middle paintbrush black.

Make sure your file is at least 300 dpi. In Photoshop, it will say "Pixels/Inch." Pixels are the same as dots. This is located under Image/Image Size. You can also go to Image/Canvas Size and make your document bigger to accommodate your whole logo.

You also might want to make this a letter-sized file. That way you can scale it down or use it for larger printed pieces. You can keep the file in RBG mode until you are ready to print.

Now it's time to add the type. Select the Text tool and click anywhere on the document. A new layer will automatically be added. Type your word, select your font, and choose your color. In our example, I typed "Ann," chose the font Stone Sans Medium, and selected the green color directly from the background. I chose all caps in this case because I wanted to emphasize the "Brushes" word the most and it looked more pleasing to have all the letters uniform. You can also add any number of special layer properties like drop shadows, embossing, etc. I decided to leave it simple.

When finished, select another tool or click on the checkmark button to indicate that you have made the changes desired. Now repeat the process for your next word. Select the type tool and click on the document. Another layer will be added. In the Ann's Brushes example, I typed in "Brushes." I chose Salto font because this is reminiscent of brushes. To emphasize the word, I made it bigger and the burgundy color, directly chosen from the background using the eyedropper tool. Now look at the words relative to your image. You may have already sketched this in your previous lesson.

Sometimes once you actually get to the layout stage, you might change your mind. In this case, I wanted the "B" to intertwine with the brushes, so I made it bigger than the rest of the word. Then I made it a drop shadow using the Layer/Layer Styles menu.

Once you have finished typing in your words, select the Move tool. That's the very first tool on the top. You also need to have the layers window open. You can open it by going to Window/Layer on your menu bar. To move your words, you need to have that layer selected on your Layer window. I do suggest typing each word into its own layer so you can have precise control of where to move it. As you are moving the words, remember to see your whole logo as a shape. In the case of Ann's Brushes, it is a rectangle.

Line up your components. For instance, the bottoms of Ann and Brushes are even. I took a guideline and dragged it down from the ruler (you can add the ruler by selecting View/Rulers on your menu bar).

Here's another example from my Wavefront logo: To line up the components vertically, I used a vertical guideline. You can see that the end of the "t", the "s", and the "n" all line up. The beginning of the "w" and the "s," all line up. The tops of the image and the top of WaveFront line up. The bottoms of the image and the "p" in Optics and Instrumentation line up. This grounds your image on an axis. This is one technique that separates excellent graphic design from shoddy design.

Be sure to zoom in on your image. Sometimes you have to go back and forth to make adjustments. There have been times I've zoomed in at 1,200 percent so I could line up things pixel by pixel!

If you want, you can incorporate your photo and slogan into the logo. Just follow the same steps. Here's an example of my logo where I have added my photo and my name.

If you want to use an actual rectangle or circle in your logo, then do this also. Choose the shape tool, click on your document, and drag your mouse to make your desired shape. You can make it any color you want.

There are any number of special options in Photoshop. One of my favorites is rendering clouds. It's very easy to make a gradient and you can blend layers together—you can make one layer transparent and bleed into the next layer!

Feathering is another great technique. For this technique, you select your picture. In the example here, my Victorian Rose logo, I made sure first that the rose artwork was in a separate layer and that the background was white. I selected the Elliptical Marquee Tool and dragged it around the rose artwork. I then selected Select/Modify/Feather and chose 16 pixels. After hit-

ting return, I chose Select/Inverse from the menu. I then hit the delete key. It created a soft feathering of the edges. In this example, I also ghosted the rose artwork layer. You do this by altering the opacity. You can find that control on your layer window up toward the top.

Keep in mind the important elements of graphic design: composition, contrast, balance, weight, etc. Make sure the final logo is appealing to your target market. Above all, make sure it is readable and communicates your message.

You might want to frequently save your document as you are working on your logo. It's always bad when you wait until the end and then something happens to freeze your computer and you lose the file! Save this logo as a Photoshop file and keep all the layers. You will use this file to make all your TIFFs, GIFs, and JPEGs.

You might try several versions and play around with the placement of your components. Just have fun and be creative! Printing it out is also very helpful. You might want to share it with a few trusted colleagues and get their opinions. Once you are satisfied with your final logo, and if you have put in an FPO image, make sure you replace it with a high resolution original. And make sure the file is at least 300 dpi or pixels/inch. Be sure to have all the relevant files together on your desktop computer in a place where you can find it easily. You may also want to put it on a CD. Think about offsite storage, too. If you should have something happen to your computer or CDs, you always want to have an extra offsite backup in case of disaster.

Because I am so terrible at remembering to backup my computers, I use an automatic Internet backup service called Carbonite. That way I always have access to my files, even if I'm just on the road and want to download my logo for any reason.

**Last Step!**

When you have created your final logo and you are satisfied with it, now it's time to output it! We will cover that in our final chapter!

# Your Selections

List below the components for your logo in order of importance.:

| Number | Components |
| --- | --- |
| | |

# Assignment

- [ ] 1 Go for it! Make your final logo as instructed in this chapter.

# Chapter Seventeen

## Step Nine to a Vacation Rental Brand that Gets Noticed—Produce It!

Congratulations! You have come a long ways in creating a vacation rental brand that gets noticed! I am positive that you created a vacation rental brand that gets noticed! Thanks for coming along on this journey with me!

So now you have your final file. You are ready to rock and roll! In this next chapter, I am going to show you how to turn your file into other files that you can use in various applications. I am going to give you a quick tutorial on how to make a business card and how to produce that through one of my favorite online printers. Remember to employ your brand strategy! The most beautiful vacation rental brand in the world won't make a bit of difference if you don't get it out in front of your target market!

This chapter will also be like a mini-graphic design tutorial. Referring back to Chapter 4 on essential elements will help you a great deal.

### Computer Files

So you have your Photoshop file (or a file from whatever program you decided to use). You have your final logo and you're ready to produce it. First you will want to make several computer files to work in a variety of applications. Generally, it is best to know exactly what size you need in each form you desire to output it in. But in this section, I will tell you how to make the different file types.

**TIFFs**—First you need to determine the size you want the logo to be. It wouldn't hurt to have a full-sized logo. If you are printing the final file, you will need this to be 300 dpi or pixels per inch. Under the layer menu, flatten the image. You can also do that by clicking on the lines on the Layer Window and scrolling down until you have selected Flatten Image. Follow the prompts.

Normally, TIFFs are for printing, so make it a CMYK file by selecting Image/Mode/CMYK. If you want it grayscale, you can select the grayscale mode and click yes when prompted. You may need to adjust some of the colors once you do that to make sure it has maximum contrast. Now select File/Save As. When prompted, select TIFF from the drop down menu.

Depending on your final destination, you may not want to imbed color profiles. I have often had compatibility issues with this selection. You will get another window. For TIFF files, I generally do not compress them and I leave it Interleaved. Select whether you want a PC or Mac file.

If you want a transparent TIFF, do not flatten the image. Instead, do a Save As. If you keep the layers choice selected, you would then also click on Save Transparency. With the Ann's Brushes logo, I saved the TIFF as a transparent file and imported it into my page layout program, QuarkXPress, I was able to put a green box behind it. This is a very important feature when laying out your marketing materials and collateral. Otherwise, you have to either build a whole file in Photoshop using layers or have a white box around everything.

When you transport these images into a page layout program like Quark, you will want to set the box color to Black, 0%. If you don't, the edges might come out jagged when printed. You also want to make sure you have the file at the exact size. It's best not to reduce it and certainly not to enlarge the file once imported into a page layout program, at least not for printed pieces like business cards and brochures.

**JPEGs**—Make sure your file is 72 dpi or pixels per inch. You can change this in the Image Size window under the Image menu.

To create a JPEG, flatten the image as you did before. Choose "Save As" and select "JPEG" in the drop down menu. Select the file quality desired, large or small, then if you want it baseline standard, optimized, or progressive. Generally, I find Baseline standard is fine.

If you want a transparent background, do not flatten the image when you do a Save As. The JPEG Options window will come up. You can choose a Matte: none, white, black, foreground, background, or custom. If you do not choose this method, there will be a white box around your image when you design it into a final piece, like a Webpage.

If you want the logo to have no background around it, you will have to build layers in Photoshop. Later on in the chapter, I will show you how to make a Web banner.

JPEGs are most useful for Web applications, especially to upload to Facebook or to a WordPress site. Be sure to note the size limitations a certain site has for a file. You may want to create several JPEGs for a range of sizes.

For JPEGs, you generally want to keep them in RGB mode. If you want to make a grayscale image, then you can do so just like in the previous example. But because these files are generally used for the Internet, it is often not necessary.

When you save a JPEG, make sure there are no spaces between words. Spaces between words will prevent your image from appearing on certain Web programs. You also have to make sure it is RGB.

GIFs—To make a transparent GIF, do not flatten the image. Click on File/Save for Web & Devices. There are many choices but none generally apply. Just hit save. In your folder, you will then have a GIF file.

Of course, including layers always increases the file size, so be aware of this. If you don't care if there's a white box around your image, then go ahead and flatten the image before you save for Web & devices.

GIFs are always in a Web Safe color mode. You don't need to do anything to change the color mode. When you convert an image to GIF, it will automatically make it 72 pixels per inch.

There are many more options in Photoshop to explore. I have been working in the program for nearly 20 years and I still am learning cool things! Just explore a little and have fun. If you make a mistake, select File/Revert and you will go back to where you started from! Just remember that you can always make an image smaller, but if you go from small to big you will lose res-

olution and the image will be blurry.

You can also make animations in Photoshop. Like I said, there are so many possibilities with this program. Explaining it all is another course in itself.

## Producing a Business Card

Okay, so you have your final logo done. You are ready to make your business card so you can get your vacation rental brand in front of your potential guests! One of the best printing services I have ever found is called OvernightPrints.com. With OvernightPrints.com, you can upload your own design, choose a template, or use their online design builder.

Beware of templates. Remember they can make your brand look like every other business card out there. I have never used the online design tool. You might try it, but I suspect you will not have as much control as designing in Adobe Photoshop. OvernightPrints will accept TIFF files and many other different kinds of files. They prefer them in CMYK mode. Just read the site to find out their technical requirements. There are very clear instructions.

You can download a starter file and use this to build your cards. You can download them in Photoshop, Illustrator, or even Microsoft Word. But Word files have to be emailed to the company for printing and you will never get the same precision in Word as in Photoshop files.

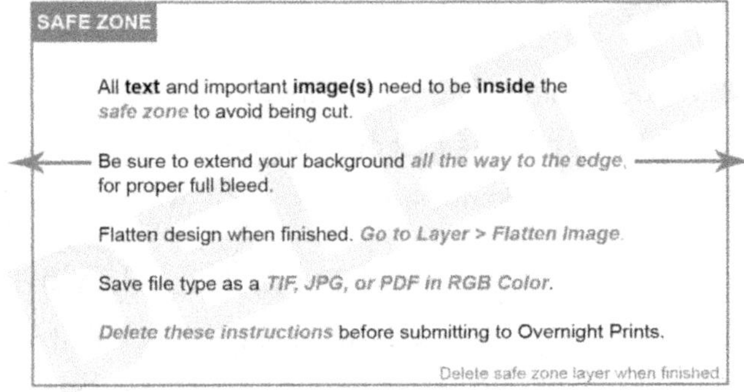

SAFE ZONE
All text and important image(s) need to be inside the safe zone to avoid being cut.
Be sure to extend your background all the way to the edge, for proper full bleed.
Flatten design when finished. Go to Layer > Flatten Image.
Save file type as a TIF, JPG, or PDF in RGB Color.
Delete these instructions before submitting to Overnight Prints.
Delete safe zone layer when finished
DELETE


If you are going to design your cards in Photoshop, download this starter file to your desktop. Open it up in your desktop.

Now it's a matter of layering different components onto your card. If you want a background, open up that image file and drag it to the starter file. It will automatically create a new layer. Make sure the background goes all the way to the edge unless you want a white border around your card. This is called "bleeding." The starter file has clear instructions about this.

You need to decide if you want your card vertical or horizontal. If you want your card vertical, then rotate the canvas 90 degrees. You can find that in Image/Rotate Canvas. Decide where you want your logo. You will want this to be the most prominent element on the page. As you can see in my example, I chose the top right-hand corner. I also made sure the logo was equidistant from the left and from the top. This is also a very important design principle. You want to make sure that you have even margins all around the card. This makes your printed piece look more professional.

The starter file is clearly marked where your safe copy lines are. When the card is printed, it will be trimmed on these lines. You do not want to have any images or text beyond these lines.

Now arrange the rest of your information where you want it. It's the same process as when you did your logo. Be sure to line up each component horizontally and vertically. You can tell that I have done so in the example here.

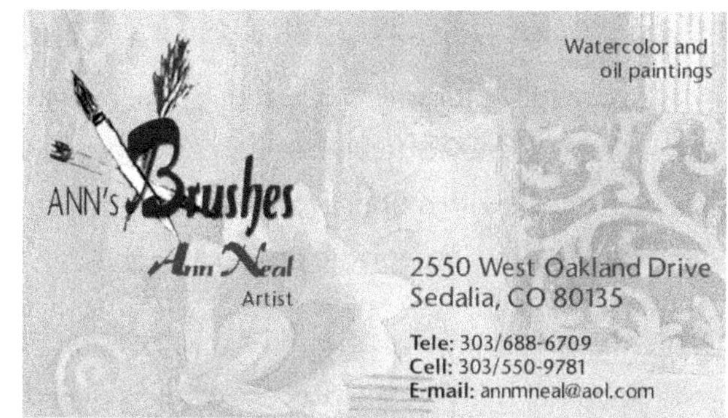


On the next page is another example of my own layout for my business card. The logo is prominent, my slogan is in the top corner, and all the contact information is below the logo. This is the card I use to let prospects, vendors, and colleagues know my contact information.

You can also add your photograph and create a tease for your mailing list. That's what I did

with the bottom business card. I decided that the main purpose when I hand out these cards is to direct them to my Website and compel them to sign up for my online newsletter.

Keep in mind that the same elements apply—balance, contrast, composition, etc. Refer back to Chapter 4 to review the essential elements.

As with most digital printers, your paper choices are limited. OvernightPrints offers 15pt card stock, gloss or matte finish coating, rounded corners, and quantities of 50 to 5,000.

Value cards can be printed on a digital press and premium cards are printed on traditional offset machines.

These cards are ideal for designing your own background and using full color. If you do not want to use full color or a background, you may want to check with your local copy shop like FedEx. I believe they offer more choices of paper. If you want your cards completely customized, check with a print broker or local offset printer. They usually have a sales representative to guides you through the process.

Also, you will need to prioritize your content. What do you want your prospects to notice first? Second? Third? Same process applies as it does your logo when it comes to choosing your most prominent features. Generally, the text is very small in business cards, the contact information as small as eight point. Your name and title should be a little bigger than the contact information.

When you have finished laying out your card, you will want to save it as a TIFF, JPG, PDF, or

anything else you desire as prescribed by OvernightPrints. You will want to make sure it is in CMYK mode and is 300 dpi or pixels per inch. You will want to flatten the image before saving. Upload it to OvernightPrints.com. You can do an online proof. Look carefully before you accept the print job! Depending on your shipping choices, you can usually have the business cards delivered to you within a week.

You can also call on local printers and get bids from them. As I mentioned before, you can work with a print broker. Printers and brokers will have prepress experts to guide you through the steps to make sure your document passes through with flying colors. There are many technical aspects to printing, so make sure you get all the information needed before you print a piece.

If you are going to do local printing, it's best to develop a relationship with a broker or a sales rep. These brokers and sales reps will get you the best deal. It's not always best to go with the cheapest option. One time I did this and did I ever regret it! It turned out that the printer was going bankrupt and couldn't even pay for his supplies. We had to yank the job and go elsewhere.

In printing, you have to make choices. You have to choose two out of the following: quality, price, or time. If you want the piece quickly and want it high quality, it's going to cost you money. If you want high quality and want it at a less expensive price, it's going to cost you time. If you want the piece for a low price and fast it's going to be poor quality.

In print design, your fonts and artwork need to be sent with your document unless you make a PDF, TIFF, or JPEG. Make sure the fonts are chosen as I described in Chapter 13. Basically, you want to choose each individual font, like Hallmark Condensed Light or Stone Sans Bold. You don't want to select the bold or italic buttons.

You also need to be aware of trapping. This is where color meets color. The trap setting in Photoshop is in the Image/Trap menu. When color meets color, generally there needs to be .214 inches around each component. If type is reversed out of a black box, for instance, it will knock out.

## Producing a Web Banner

Now let's talk about the other way you will want to produce your logo—in a Web banner. Photoshop is an ideal program for doing this. Create a new file and make it the banner size you desire. For my blog, I made it 940 by 198 pixels. Generally, Web files are measured in pixels rather than inches. Just find out what the banner size requirements are, like in WordPress. You also want to set it at 72 pixels per inch. RGB colors are your best mode choice.

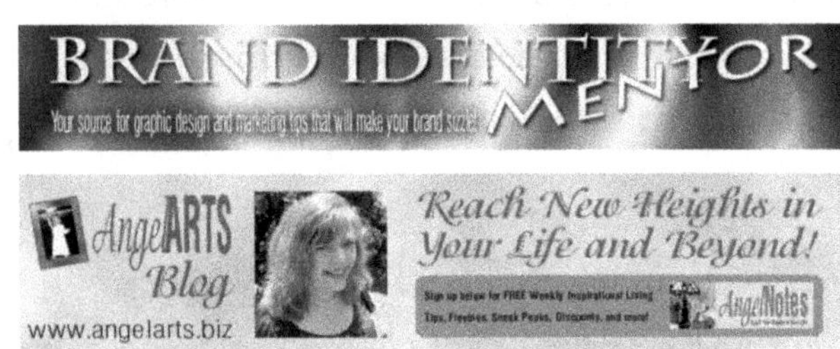


Decide what you want your background to be. For my branding blog, I used the flame image that is central to the brand. For my regular AngelArts blog, I used the render clouds filter to make a pink cloud. This also goes along with my branding.

Make your background and then lay out your other components, piece by piece. The same design principles apply. Make sure your logo and photo are prominent. As in the case of WordPress, your banner can have the title of your blog while the software itself contains your logo. See the example to the right.

Save your completed file as a JPEG or GIF and upload it to your site or incorporate it into your Web page layout. You can use this process to design many Web banners, including newsletter mastheads (titles), animated ads, banner ads, button ads, and Web buttons.

## Producing a Web Banner

So you've made it through this course and you've decided you really do not want to do your

own graphic design. Don't worry. There are many options available. You now have the tools available to manage incredible vacation rental branding products! If you don't feel it's worth your time to learn the mechanics of graphic design, then you may want to hire it out.

If you are looking for something low cost, you can use a service like 99Designs. This service charges around $295 for logo design. It is a contest between several designers and you choose your favorite one. Now these designers may not be of ad agency quality because they are competing with each other, but because you have gone through this course, you will get a much better product.

There are also services like guru.com or freelance.com. You can bid out your job at your budget price and you will receive several proposals from designers. There are also ways to hire out graphic design to overseas workers, such as in the Philippines.

Of course, you can hire an ad agency. These designers will cost at least $100 per hour. They usually will give you a free estimate and charge you by the project. Independent freelance designers are also a more affordable way to go if you want high quality design. As a freelance designer myself, I give free initial consultations, written estimates, and I charge by the project. Good designers will have you sign a contract or working agreement. The most professional ones will give you a proposal. This is what I always do. I have my clients pay me a deposit and then pay the remainder upon final approval of the job and upon final production of their piece. If I estimate too low for the job, then it is my fault and I eat the charge. I also make it very clear to my client that if they change the parameters of the job, I will have to charge accordingly. This is standard practice and usually requires what is called a change order.

Remember that your vacation rental brand is your most important asset. Corporations pay tens of thousands of dollars to professional ad agencies for graphic design. If you think cheap, you will get cheap. Expand your thinking and you will expand your vacation rental business!

### I Would Love To Work With You!

If you've decided to hire out the graphic design, why not consider working with someone you

know and trust? Me! I will give a credit to any client who has read this book! So if you would like a free initial consultation and free written estimate, you can always contact me at 719-785-4814 or info@angelarts.biz. I would love to work with you!

You can also become a Facebook fan at Brand Identity Quest. On my Brand Identity Quest page, you will find updates on upcoming courses. You can also find me on my blog at www.BrandIdentityMentor.com and if you want to take a look at my advanced webinar and mentor programs, check www.BrandIdentityMentorPrograms.com.

I will be doing more detailed training on print design, Photoshop mechanics, and Quark mechanics. Deborah and I will also have training on a periodic basis, so sign up for our mailing list to get notification of our events.

Thanks for journeying with me in unmasking your authentic identity! If you would like to be a featured student and show off your work, please contact me! I would love to have your testimonial! And of course I will link to your Website! As you apply these lessons learned through this book, I am confident that you will have a vacation rental brand that gets noticed!

# *Assignment*

- [ ] 1 Produce your vacation rental logo into your desired pieces, whether business cards, banners, postcards, or whatever you choose. Just remember to ask for the technical requirements and be sure you produce the file to their standards.

# Chapter Eighteen
## The Website Brand

OK. Now you have your logo, your identity, and branding strategy. Finally, you are in the position to build your own site. Well maybe...or maybe not. Since you are listed on quite a few vacation rental sites, you might question if you really need your own "company" site.

Your vacation rental property is listed with all the major paid sites, VRBO, Homeaway, Vacation Rental.com, etc. You need to spend money to make money, right? But where does it end? I was spending nearly $5,000 a year on listing my vacation rental on these sites. If you are like me, I questioned if should I invest even more in building my own vacation business website? How could I compete with these major sites?

After years in the vacation rental business, I realized the point was not to compete with the "big boys," but to expand on what they do. Aside from guests expecting it, a "company site" builds credibility. Here are some benefits to having one:

- **Get More Bookings:** When a potential guest calls on a listing, you may immediately send him to your website while talking to him. In the e-mails you send out, always provide a link to your site. Whisk the potential guest away from "the big search sites," where all the other listings are! Get more bookings by providing detailed information to simplify the decision-making process. Giving customers a link to your site saves them from the confusion of too many choices!
- **Controlled Information:** On your site, you may provide slide shows, videos, testimonials,

and map links to "the area" for free. Many major listing sites do not allow links to your site or slide show without an extra charge! I have concerns with providing the exact address of vacation properties, as some major listing sites are pressuring owners to do. Publicly posting an exact address on the Internet is a safety and privacy issue for guests, neighbors, and owners. More on that in my book, *VROM—Vacation Rental Owner's Manual.*

- Save Money: Cut the cost of advertising on "must-do" listing sites, by including "extras" such as slide shows, videos, map links, local tourist info, and unlimited photos on your site. Don't want to learn HTML or become a website designer? You can build an instant vacation rental website. The money you save by eliminating the "extra charges" from paid listing(s) can fund your own site. Forget the learning curve, and simply upload property photos. To get the look and feel of a professional site, use automated vacation rental website as an inexpensive, quick, and easy solution for building your own site.

### How to Build a Website for Almost Free

Obviously you can hire someone to build a website for you, but this can be very costly and time consuming if you do not get the right website designer. There is also a wide range of skills between different website designers, and unless you practically know how to build your own site, you might find yourself a victim of those who overcharge and under deliver. "You don't know what you don't know," can be costly in this kind of situation. So let's get you educated before you make some website decisions.

Definitions and Simplifications—First of all, you've already done enough work getting your vacation rental ready, so let's keep it simple. Luckily it's pretty simple to build sites for Vacation Rental. Most of your budget is best invested in photographs, photographs, and photographs. I actually recommend hiring a professional photographer (or trade for a few weeks stay in your vacation rental for a photographer's work) to take "glamor photos" of your home inside and out. Make sure to include photos of local tourist attractions that your guests can visit. As long as you have beautiful photos, the rest of the site will go almost unnoticed. I was able to get one of my clients (vacation rental consultations) a world-class photographer to shoot $7,000 worth of HIGH-end photos in exchange for a few week's stay. Wow. What an incredible difference professional photos make. (www.SantaBarbaraVacationRentals.us)

A couple of definitions that will help you are: the World Wide Web, (www), domain name, hosting site, and website. Think of the World Wide Web (www) as virtual real estate, more specifically, virtual land. The World Wide Web is the space; the domain is the address in the space. A domain name is like a PO box; it gives a location of where your piece of virtual real estate is located. A person can type the domain name into the computer's browser and arrive at your site. The website is the "home"—the improvements that you build onto the virtual real estate.

Websites are now being given appraisals on their worth based on a number of factors. The hosting company is like a virtual landlord. You rent (or you may own if you want to be in the hosting company business) virtual space on the World Wide Web, but there are costs associated with keeping that area of the web functioning. So you rent the virtual space from a hosting company. Once you have that space set aside, you are able to define it by forwarding your domain name to that space. The name servers (of the hosting company) tell computers where to go when looking for your site. So those are the basic terminologies of the world of Internet commerce.

**Domain Name Selection and SEO**—It's one thing to build a website and it is yet another for people to visit it...and stay for a while! That will be the next challenge you will want to overcome. The art and science of being found on the web is often referred to as SEO (Search Engine Optimization). This means that you build a website and its components to be found on Google, Bing, Yahoo, and all the search engines where people are looking for your products or services. There are about 10 key elements that work together to make it possible to be found near the top of the search engines for certain keywords. Companies pay six figure incomes to full time staffs to do SEO for their brand. But you too, can be found on the web by paying attention to a few key things, and building that into your branding and your SEO.

The single most important thing that will help you be found in search engine searches is the selection of the domain name. In the name of simplicity, value, and effectiveness; I suggest that

you get two domain names...one that reflects the area where your property is located and one that is the actual name of your vacation rental. For one of my clients I was able to get www.SantaBarbaraVacationRentals.us and after a year's activity, when people type in Santa Barbara vacation rentals, his site can be found. But now that he has a lot of repeat customers, we also use the domain name, www.Farosmontecitoretreat.com because customers know his brand now. I suggest you use both. You can build your site on one domain, and forward the other to the site, so that both names will bring a person to your site. This is key information that will save and make you thousands of dollars in SEO, if you do these simple things in the very beginning.

The second most important thing that will help you to be found on the search engines, is to add a guest book feature to your website, and do whatever you can to get your guests to go to your site and write a review. Give them a free incentive of some type. We talked about this in the chapter on Promotional Products branding. This creates new content on a regular basis, without you having to actually write a blog every day or every week, and you will get the new content and activity on your site that the search engines like to see. If they see new content and activity they will rank your site higher and higher, which in turn will create new content and new activity! We will talk about how to add a guest book feature a little later.

### Simple Fast Approach with Minimal Cost

There are a couple of approaches. If you want to go super simple, and super quick, there is a service that specializes in vacation rental sites, and only charges about $35 a year for a vacation rental template site. It will not have as much flexibility as the site would if you built your own, but in the interest of getting something up right away, and if you know very little about building a site, I suggest going with this option. I will explain later how to set up a domain name that will forward to the site, so that you can include your branding words in the domain name. This is critical to beginning to build time on the Web with your domain name, so that the search engines will find it as your vacation rental business grows, and return guests and referrals begin to look for you.

### Build Your Own for Free

The best option if you are up for it, is to build your "company" website for almost free. There is a 100% free option using WordPress, which is one of the best website softwares available and it's shareware, proven over the years. There are a couple of approaches you can take on this one. There's a free WordPress venue, which is sitting on the WordPress hosting site. However, if you do this, it is a bit risky, because WordPress may shut your site down if they think it's commercial. I have had several sites that they shut down, one was non-profit, but they deemed it was commercial. To prevent losing everything you've developed, I suggest you use the Tools options and save your website to a flash drive or burn it to a DVD just in case. Saving your work someplace beside your computer is a good practice anyway.

For a little more money, and a little more security, you may buy hosting from a number of hosting companies. I suggest GoDaddy, because they have 24-hour customer service, and it's good! Also they have WordPress software as an option and it's the best for building sites for the following reasons:

- Easily recognized by search engines, for good, no cost SEO recognition.
- Easy to build, user friendly, similar to Microsoft Office.
- Tutorials available on YouTube, or other sources such as Lynda.com.
- If you hire someone to build it, it's simple enough that you can do your own updates, sales, or changes without paying over and over for updates.
- It's easy to add on plugins for even more user interactive features such as guest book, social networking features, and the ability to add sign up forms.

Hosting with GoDaddy with WordPress available as software for building your site will run about $5 a month. You can get coupons and that will reduce the cost to about $50 a year. Then you will need to purchase two domain names, about $7.49 each year using coupons that can be found on Google. It's best to buy the domain names for two years in a row, since that is a third factor for helping get higher search engine rankings. If you use GoDaddy, the domain can be simply set up to their hosting, as well as the name servers, as it is all with the same company.

So for under $100 a year, you can have your own website at your fingertips. Check with

www.vacationrentalguru.org for seminars and workshops on how to build a strong vacation rental site. If you need a vacation rental consultant or vacation rental website consultant check on our site to reach out for Deborah Nelson's consulting rates and availability.

# Assignment

- [ ] 1 Choose a domain name for your vacation rental site. Check on GoDaddy or other hosting site for availability.

- [ ] 2 Consider purchasing a hosting account through GoDaddy (or Hostgator.com is another very good site) and setting up a WordPress account.

# Chapter Nineteen
## Intellectual Property

No discussion of branding is complete without a basic understanding of intellectual property rights. Investing in and creating a brand builds value that can translate into steady cash flow. Starting with a business concept and a mission and vision statement, you develop a logo, website presence, spread the word with social networking, and use other methods of positioning the brand as one that is trusted and known in your circle of influence. It costs money and takes time to build a brand.

Think of real estate. When people first started claiming their rights to land in the early settlement years of the United States, they would stake a claim and literally put a stake into the land. At some point a survey was done and the survey would legally describe the location, size, and scope of the claimed land. Based on the description of the land, a title would be issued and ownership based on that title was then filed and authenticated by the local government. Ownership was defined, and value established.

The same sort of process goes on with intellectual property. Law defines intellectual property in one of three basic legal methods: copyrights, trademarks, and patents. Although not yet recognized as intellectual property, there is also a recent development in modern intellectual property, which is a domain name defined on the World Wide Web. In this chapter we will also address the domain name as it relates to trademarks and intellectual property.

## Copyrights

Copyrights relate to artistic property such as original photography, writing, illustrations, paintings, graphic designs, maps, and original creative works, such as song lyrics, music, poetry, an article, curriculum, or a book. It's easy to copyright your work by going to www.uspto.com and uploading your document. For those in the business, this can be time consuming, and common law does more or less assume that if your original work is published there is a copyright. It's best to put your copyright with a small "c" and a circle around it (©) along with your name and date when publishing any work. Additionally, the reason it may be important to register your copyrighted works with the U.S. Patent and Trademark Office (USPTO), is if you anticipate a lawsuit or suspect other business entities may want to use your work. Just because you have a trademark, copyright, or patent, doesn't guarantee that someone won't plagiarize your work. However, if you end up in court for theft of intellectual property, your settlement will be much higher if you have an officially registered copyright on the item in question.

## Patents and Patents Pending

Patents and patents pending are more complicated. Most people hire patent attorneys to submit these. However, if you would like to have one year of breathing room, you may apply for a patent pending—which is quite simple. The application fee is $80. Once you have described your unique invention, and filled out the patent pending paperwork (a few pages); then you can mail it *express mail* and keep the receipt to show it was filed with the USPTO. Once they accept your form, you can claim patent pending status, and be protected for your invention while you are introducing it to the world on a website.

## Registered Trademarks

Trademarks are fairly simple a well. Trademark is for the name of your brand, website, or company. You can go online to the www.USPTO.com website, and learn how to apply for a trademark. I recommend that if you are any good with paperwork and red tape, it's pretty easy. The fee is $325. You will do a search in the database first to make sure no one else already owns the trademark. There are two types of trademarks, one is the "word" trademark and the other is the "mark" trademark. I always file for the "word" trademark first, and then later file for the mark. This is because you may change your logo a few times in the process of bringing up your business, and you would have to go through this process every time you wanted to change your trademark "mark," which would be costly and time consuming. You are allowed to use the symbols ™ for your trademark without applying but you cannot use the symbols ® for registered trademarked unless you actually have gone through the process with the United States Government and have been approved for that trademark.

### Domain Names and Trademark Relationship

There is new legislation regarding trademarks and domain names. It is expected that if you have a trademark you will also own that domain name. The domain name is almost a modern trademark and once you have that domain name, it's now against federal law for anyone to obtain your domain name that is a registered trademark for the purpose of making money from it! That domain name belongs to you (if you have made it a registered trademark). It is important to trademark those very same words that are in your domain name, so that no one could ever try to buy and sell your domain and put a huge price tag on it. If you are ahead of the game, you can avert this potential danger.

### The Value of Intellectual Property

Even though you can't always see it, intellectual property has value, but if you don't define it and protect it, anyone can take it and use it. After you may have spent years developing a unique product, service, or brand, and then someone capitalizes on your hard work, it can be devastating.  So take the time to understand your options in protecting your intellectual property more thoroughly. A great way to learn more about these is to go to www.USPTO.com and watch their videos and read all their information. And even better, is to read and refer to Gary Nolo legal books, which teach you how to apply for trademarks, patents, and copyrights without a lawyer. With a little study, you can save thousands of dollars in attorney fees, and the heartbreak of someone else trading on your unprotected brand, or product.

## No Guarantees

If you have copyrights, patents, or trademarks there is no guarantee that your intellectual property or brand will not be stolen, used, or copied. But it's a bit like the laptop sitting on the seat of an unlocked car vs. the laptop that is in a case, locked up in the trunk, and out of sight. If you use patents, copyrights, and registered trademarks, your intellectual property is less likely to be stolen, or wrongly used. You are putting sort of a lock on your intellectual brand or property when you apply these processes to your work. In the end, if someone does wrongfully use your brand, or unique product, or process, you will need to decide if you want to pursue them legally. But if you clearly have the intellectual property registration, you can write a cease-and-desist letter, and they will likely stop. You will need to decide if they have unfairly benefited by using your intellectual property, and weigh out if it is worth it to become involved in a lengthy court battle, asking for your due compensation. Often, if your case is strong there can be an out of court settlement, and if you have all your paperwork, and there is a clear violation, and financial benefit, you may be able to retain an attorney who will work for a percentage of the settlement, thus avoiding any out-of-pocket legal expenses.

## Closing Thoughts

Now we, your authors, thank you for joining us on this journey. You have come a long ways: you've identified your strengths, weaknesses, goals, and more; chosen your vacation rental name if you didn't already have one; learned about the essential elements of design; created a brand strategy; selected your images, fonts, and colors; created a logo; and produced it into business cards, Web banners, Websites, and more! You should now have the tools to make an excellent brand as well as a way to get your brand in front of potential guests.

May your vacation rental brand truly get noticed and may your bookings soar!

# Assignment

- ☐ 1 Consider the benefits of trademarking your vacation rental brand.

- ☐ 2 Please share your completed brands with us! You can email them to info@vacation-rentalguru.org! We would love to see what you come up with!

# About Vacation Rental GURUS

**Deborah S. Nelson** and **Dana Susan Beasley** are the creators of Vacation Rental Gurus. Dedicated to producing effective and strategic resources for vacation rental owners, Deborah and Dana delight in sharing their experiences in the business, helping others avoid costly mistakes and bringing the industry to a new level of professionalism.

If you like this book, you'll love Deborah and Dana's other products that will give you practical guidance as a vacation rental owner.

**Deborah,** an entrepreneurial writer and marketer with over 20 years experience, has marketed multiple vacation rental properties at a time. She fell into the vacation rental business by accident, when Deborah realized that renting her townhome in Colorado would help pay her daughter's way to studying in Europe for college. Through that experience, she learned the art of marketing vacation rentals and Vacation Suites Global (www.vacationsuitesglobal.com), her vacation rental marketing company, was born.

Deborah has authored and published 10 books available at Author Your Dreams (www.authoryourdreams.com) and is the owner of The Adstuff Company, (www.theadstuffcompany.com) a logo branded products company specializing in branded items.

**Dana,** a publisher, writer, and graphic artist, started a vacation rental with her husband. Together, they remodeled an 1898 Victorian home and made it into a spectacular place for guests to enjoy. With Dana's hospitality sense and acumen for interior design and her hus-

band's expertise in remodeling, they created a vacationer's dream. Their guest book bursts with glowing reports from satisfied customers!

Owner of AngelArts (www.angelarts.biz), a creative arts agency and publishing house, Dana delights in using her graphic design and writing skills to create excellent online resources and unique products. She also homeschools her school-aged child.

She is the creator of Brand Identity Quest, an extensive course on how to build brands that sizzle.

You can learn more about Deborah and Dana's products at www.VacationRentalGuru.org.

# Notes

## Do-It-Yourself Vacation Rental Branding Sources


### Chapter Two

1. Rose DeNeve, *The Designer's Guide to Creating Corporate I.D. Systems for Companies of all type and sizes* (Cincinnati, Ohio: North Light Books, 1992), 7–9.

### Chapter Three

1. Raleigh Pinskey, *101 Ways to Promote Yourself* (New York, New York: Avon Books, 1997), 3.

### Chapter Ten

1. Rose DeNeve, *The Designer's Guide to Creating Corporate I.D. Systems for Companies of all type and sizes* (Cincinnati, Ohio: North Light Books, 1992), 38–39.
2. Raleigh Pinskey, *101 Ways to Promote Yourself* (New York, New York: Avon Books, 1997), 3.
3. Rose DeNeve, *The Designer's Guide to Creating Corporate I.D. Systems for Companies of all type and sizes* (Cincinnati, Ohio: North Light Books, 1992), 41.
4. Rose DeNeve, *The Designer's Guide to Creating Corporate I.D. Systems for Companies of all type and sizes* (Cincinnati, Ohio: North Light Books, 1992), 41.
5. Rose DeNeve, *The Designer's Guide to Creating Corporate I.D. Systems for Companies of all type and sizes* (Cincinnati, Ohio: North Light Books, 1992), 41.

# WANT MORE ADVANCED COACHING FOR YOUR VACATION RENTAL BRAND?

JOIN ONE OF DANA'S ONLINE COACHING AND MENTORING PROGRAMS!

- INTENSIVE TRAINING
- LIVE TUTORIALS
- CASE STUDY OF A BRAND IN PROGRESS
- INTERACTIVE WORKSHOP FORMAT
- MORE SECRETS, TIPS, AND TRICKS!
- LIVE Q&A SESSIONS!

WWW.BRANDIDENTITYMENTORPROGRAMS.COM

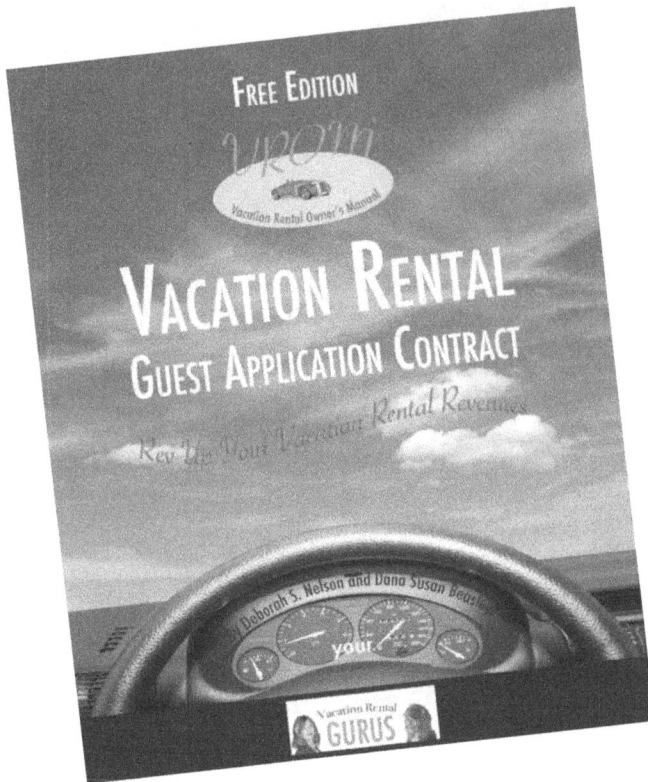

www.ingramcontent.com/pod-product-compliance
Lightning Source LLC
Chambersburg PA
CBHW062025210326
41519CB00060B/7100

* 9 7 8 0 6 1 5 6 0 1 9 3 9 *